The Reluctant Leader

The Reluctant Leader:

Coming out of the Shadows

Peter Shaw
and Hilary Douglas

CANTERBURY
PRESS
Norwich

First published in 2016 by the Canterbury Press Norwich
Editorial office
3rd Floor, Invicta House
108–114 Golden Lane
London EC1Y 0TG, UK

Canterbury Press is an imprint of Hymns Ancient & Modern Ltd (a
registered charity)
13A Hellesdon Park Road, Norwich,
Norfolk NR6 5DR, UK

www.canterburypress.co.uk

British Library Cataloguing in Publication data

A catalogue record for this book is available
from the British Library

978 1 84825 875 4

Typeset by Rebecca Goldsmith

Printed and bound in Great Britain by
CPI Group (UK) Croydon

Contents

Dedicated to our families and friends,
whose love and support mean so much.

Acknowledgements

We both want to acknowledge the people who believed in us early in our careers. Clive Booth and Nick Stuart taught Hilary about fresh ways of looking at challenges and staying resilient, possibly without realizing that was what they were doing. Dorothy White proved there was a place for mothers at the top, at a time when there were few role models. For Peter, it was James Hamilton and Mark Carlisle who pushed him to overcome reluctance as a Yorkshire lad to contribute confidently in a range of settings.

We want to thank all the individuals and teams we have worked with as coaches. Overcoming reluctance has often been a strong theme of our conversations. We have been impressed by the willingness of so many people to address this challenge openly and constructively.

Una O'Brien, a former Permanent Secretary at the Department of Health, offered the original idea for this book. Una saw reluctance as both friend and foe. Reluctance can stop you from rushing in too fast, but it can hold you back from giving of your best. Una has been very supportive of the approaches we have developed in this book.

We are grateful to Caroline Gardner for writing a foreword which draws from her own leadership journey to become Auditor General for Scotland.

We are grateful to Christine Smith who recognized the importance of this theme and commissioned us to write this book. She is always perceptive and supportive as a commissioning editor. Jackie Tookey has typed the text with her normal thoroughness and care. Sonia John-Lewis has managed our diaries to allow time for the writing. Our colleagues at Praesta Partners have always been a valuable source of ideas.

Our families have been great sources of encouragement, as ever. We could not have written the book without their support.

The royalties from this book will go to the British Red Cross, to support their work with people in crisis in the UK and across the world.

Foreword

When I became Auditor General for Scotland I was surprised how much I enjoyed the CEO part of my role. The satisfaction came from believing wholeheartedly in the goals of the organisation and learning how to remain true to myself as a leader. I was able to draw on a wide range of previous experiences that helped to shape how I wanted to 'be' as the CEO.

When you take on a leadership role be ready to be surprised by your reaction. There will be daunting moments and joyful moments. You will be surprised by how people listen to you and are influenced by you. You will delight in watching people gain in confidence and effectiveness. You will get a lot of satisfaction through what you are able to initiate.

Moving into a bigger leadership role gives you the chance to be the leader you want to be. Trust in your ability to do the role in your way – received wisdom about how leadership 'should' be done is not always right. Don't pretend to be someone you're not.

Leaders who don't fit the stereotypes can be particularly effective. They build trust and goodwill, and model possibilities for others who don't fit the mould. You can remain yourself and be true to your values, and be more effective as a result.

Those who are reluctant or hesitant to take on leadership roles will often make the best leaders, as they bring more self- awareness and a good dose of humility. The reluctant leader is more likely to have thought through the consequences of their actions and be ready for a range of opportunities and risks.

Success comes through a combination of self-reflection and practical action. It flows from a willingness to test out ideas and keep learning from what works well. An element of self doubt means you are more likely to plan your interventions carefully.

This book is an excellent quarry of ideas and practical steps for those thinking of taking the plunge into a bigger leadership role. It sets out worthwhile approaches to stepping out of the shadows so you make the most of your opportunities to engage and deliver as a leader.

Peter Shaw and Hilary Douglas bring a wealth of insight that infuses the book. They draw on their personal experience of overcoming elements of self-doubt as leaders in the early stages of their careers, which prepared them to become Director Generals in Government and trustees of significant charities. They have both worked as coaches with many leaders who have been hesitant or unsure: they have taken delight in the way these individuals have become authentic, confident and influential leaders.

Read this book ready to be engaged. Be open to using your reluctance or self-doubt as a resource to help you become the best leader you can be. Be ready to be surprised by what you are capable of.

Caroline Gardner
Auditor General for Scotland
Edinburgh

About the authors

Hilary Douglas

Hilary Douglas coaches leaders and potential leaders from a wide variety of sectors, backgrounds and cultures. She works with them one to one, and in teams and groups. Time and again, she finds that talented people are held back by the beliefs they hold about themselves. Hence her interest in the theme of this book.

Hilary is co-author of a report by Praesta Partners on the issues that senior women bring to coaching. She has also written a Praesta booklet on what makes a successful Chair of a public sector Board.

In Hilary's first career, she led on all aspects of organizational change, leadership development, corporate services and infrastructure as a Board member of several different UK Government Departments. She has been a member of a school governing body, and a trustee of various charities. She is currently a trustee and Vice-Chair on the Board of the British Red Cross.

Peter Shaw

Peter Shaw has coached individuals, senior teams and groups across six continents. He is a Visiting Professor in leadership development at Newcastle University, Chester University and St John's College, Durham University. He teaches regularly at Regent College, Vancouver.

He has written 22 books on aspects of leadership including:

Sustaining Leadership, 2014, Canterbury Press.
100 Great Team Effectiveness Ideas, 2015, Marshall
  Cavendish.
100 Great Building Success Ideas, 2016, Marshall Cavendish.

Peter's first career was in the UK Government where he worked in five Government Departments and held three Director General posts. Peter has been a member of governing bodies in higher and further education. He is a Licensed Lay Minister (Reader) in the Anglican Church and plays an active role in the Church of England at parish, diocesan and national levels. He holds a Doctorate in Leadership Development from Chester University and was awarded an Honorary Doctorate by Durham University for his 'outstanding service to public life'.

Hilary and Peter work together on a wide range of coaching assignments with individuals, teams and groups in the public, private and voluntary sectors. They bring complementary skills and backgrounds. The focus in their coaching work is to enable individuals and teams to be the best they can be. Often part of their work is enabling individuals and teams to overcome the reluctance that is holding them back and to become more confident and better equipped to lead effectively through demanding situations. Their contact details are peter.shaw@praesta.com and hilary.douglas@praesta.com.

Introduction

What is holding you back from being the leader you could be? What might happen if you looked at yourself and the opportunities available to you in a different way? How might you be liberated from your inhibitions, so you can be more confident and adventurous?

This book is for those who hold back from seeking leadership responsibilities and those who are in leadership roles but find it difficult to exercise their full leadership influence and authority. It encourages you to look through a different lens at what might be possible. It offers you insights about how to manage your brain and suggests approaches that have worked for leaders in different spheres. It gives you tools and techniques that can be applied in a variety of settings.

Our aim is to help you handle your blind spots and address your anxieties. The book will help you see events from other people's perspectives so you can intervene with a greater degree of confidence. It will help you understand more about your impact on others.

Addressing and overcoming reluctance has been a consistent theme in our coaching work with leaders and emerging leaders. The ideas in this book therefore flow from many hours of conversations with reluctant leaders in the voluntary, private and public sectors. The ideas are relevant to leaders and emerging leaders in many different contexts, organizations, cultures and countries.

We hope the book will be useful for those who are seeking to grow the leadership potential of the people who work for them, whether as individuals or as a team. It could also be useful to those who have no wish to lead, but need to manage upwards.

We look first at why good leadership matters and how you can better understand your emotional reactions to work challenges. We look at 'taking the plunge' in overcoming a reluctance to take on leadership roles. We explore what it means for leaders to 'come out of the shadows' if they are finding it hard to assert their contribution and authority.

As we were finalizing the book, the UK electorate voted by a narrow margin to leave the European Union. Greater uncertainty has been added to an already uncertain world. Good leadership will be even more important in every sphere of life.

We conclude with a suggested ten next steps as a prompt for thought and action. We will be delighted if these are helpful in your leadership journey.

Peter Shaw   Hilary Douglas

Godalming, Surrey   *London*

PART ONE

Understand the context

This section explores why good leadership matters, and why we may owe it to others, as much as to ourselves, to use our leadership potential to the full. It describes how the human brain reacts to the challenges of life and how we can learn to manage our emotions, rather than letting them manage us.

Chapters 1 and 2 provide the background to much of what is said in Parts 2 and 3. If you are dipping into the later chapters, we would encourage you to read these two chapters first.

1

Believe that good leadership matters

Leading well is hard work. This chapter is about why the effort is worth it, and why society needs leaders of all kinds, not just those who fit the charismatic stereotype. By denying your leadership potential, you may be depriving others as well as yourself.

Societies and communities need successful leaders at all levels and in all types of organization. Most of us want to feel that we are well led, because the consequences of poor or malevolent leadership are profound. Leadership may come from a team, or through a hierarchy, but without it there is little sense of direction or purpose. At best, there is drift. At worst – and particularly if leadership is disputed – there is chaos.

You may think you can do little to influence the quality of leadership in the modern world, but leadership matters in the local as much as the global context. Research shows that the key ingredient of a successful school is good leadership. Faith communities look to their leaders to help them define their values and live by them. There is evidence that UK productivity would be higher if there were more effective leaders at every level in companies and public services.

We are not saying that everyone is suited to leading people or organizations. You are bound to know people who are dedicated to a solo career, or want to work for themselves. Their vocation may lie in serving and praying for others, in reaching peak performance in their chosen field, or in building a business based solely on their personal expertise. They may still have the opportunity to show personal leadership in the sense of standing up for what they believe in, but that is not the focus of this book.

Our focus in this book is on people who have the potential to contribute as leaders of others, and whose potential, for whatever reason, is not being realized.

Sometimes the barriers lie in the environment. In many societies and organizations, women still find it harder to succeed, as do people from minority groups of all kinds. The current leaders of those societies and organizations need to recognize they are missing out on a huge amount of talent. If they are providing services to customers or citizens, they are also missing insight into how those customers think.

Often it is the potential leaders themselves who are reluctant to step forward. There may be personal circumstances such as location or caring responsibilities, which mean that the individual makes a conscious choice to wait. More frequently, we hear people say they lack confidence. They cannot imagine filling the shoes of the people above them. They fear failure and living with the consequences of their decisions. They overestimate their limitations and underestimate their strengths.

It is often a revelation for talented people to hear that they are not alone in feeling like this. Even among highly successful leaders, we meet many who have battled with self-doubt throughout their career, and may still believe that it is only a matter of time before they are found out. Just try googling 'imposter syndrome'.

Many high achievers are perfectionists who are their own worst critics. They blame themselves whenever something goes wrong, rather than looking for the learning. They may also assume that leaders have to be supremely self-confident to succeed. They have a mental picture of a great leader inspiring the troops to battle and cannot identify with this image.

There is plenty of evidence that a range of leadership styles are needed in our complex modern society. The most effective leaders are self-aware and consciously flex their style according to circumstances. A command and control approach may be essential in a military campaign or a peacetime emergency, because there is no time to debate what to do. Yet even then, it can make a huge difference if the leader has already gained people's trust in their ability to decide well. Heroic leaders remain heroic only for as long as they take their people with them.

The impact of the charismatic leader can be negative as often as it is positive. Such a leader is often ego-driven and convinced that he or she is always right, with the consequence that others' contributions are suppressed. They may micro manage and stifle innovation. They may use hierarchy to create a compliance culture. Are you more motivated by a leader whose priority is their personal image, or a leader who cares about stretching everyone to make the best possible contribution?

If the leader creates an environment where everyone invests in success, it is less lonely at the top. The ultimate responsibility for decisions still lies with that leader, but they accept that they don't know everything, and are skilled at asking the right questions. They are attentive listeners and they readily drop their own ideas if they believe someone has come up with something better.

Enabling leaders are not a soft touch. They simply recognize they are more likely to achieve great results by creating an environment where talent can flourish. They appreciate that different people have different motivations and learning styles, and they adapt their approach to fit. They become fascinated by finding the keys to unlocking potential.

Perfectionism is still a driver for such leaders, but it is about continuous improvement and learning for the whole organization. There is less pressure to be perfect as an individual. As one of our clients once put it: 'It was a breakthrough when I realized this wasn't all about me.'

If you believe that good leadership matters, ask yourself how you could help multiply the energy in your organization. Be honest with yourself about the difference you want to make, and the value you could bring. Then explore what is holding you back. How likely is it that your worst fears would come about? What could you do to make it less likely that they will, and to build your resilience for the inevitable knocks of life?

We hope that some of the ideas in this book will help you overcome any hesitation and step confidently into leadership. There is a consistent theme around recognizing and managing negative emotions in yourself and others, and that is what the next chapter is about.

For reflection

- What does good leadership mean to you? Where have you seen it and what is the difference that it makes?

- Could you be a multiplier of energy, who helps others to grow and contribute?

- Do you know what is holding you back? Can you write it down or say it out loud? What would help you to move forward?

2

Understand your brain

Carl had been in his role as Deputy Headteacher for a couple of years. It meant a lot to him that he received good feedback from the Head, who had supported and mentored him as his responsibilities grew. At his most recent appraisal the Head had suggested Carl should start applying for headships. He felt a rising sense of panic as she was speaking and gave her a firm message that this was not for him.

Subsequently Carl talked to a trusted friend about his reaction. He realized there had always been an older, more experienced, person to turn to in his life. It gave him a sense of security to know that the Head was there if he needed her advice, and that she would take any decision that felt too big for him. The idea that he could take sole responsibility for running a school made him feel deeply insecure. He had discounted the fact that he rarely needed advice these days, and had acted up several times in the Head's absence. He began to think more rationally about the extra training or experience he might need to make himself fully ready for a headship application.

Carl's friend helped him to see that his sense of reluctance came from within. The prospect of promotion can spark delight in one person and anxiety in another, even when they are equally capable. You might say it is a matter of confidence, but what is confidence about? It is worth pausing for a moment to think about the human brain – your brain – and how it works.

The sense of anxiety about a new challenge is driven by the part of your brain which works with instinct and emotion. It has not evolved much since our ape ancestors. It acts as though we are still trying to survive in the jungle, so your brain fears the unknown, and prepares for the worst to happen. It sees terrible consequences in making a wrong decision and feels safest doing familiar things, where it has a degree of control. The brain may perceive danger where there is none, because something about the current situation reminds it of a bad experience. The brain feels a need to protect the herd, and wants to please the bigger beasts, thinking this is crucial to survival.

The emotional brain always responds faster to events than the part of the brain which produces rational thought. That is a scientific fact, with good reasons why we have evolved this way. There is no time to think if a dangerous animal, or nowadays a fast car, is bearing down on you: you get yourself out of harm's way. However, there are lots of situations in the modern world where you can't and don't allow your emotions to run away with you. Most of us realize from an early age that we must manage our emotions to be acceptable to the society we live in. If children are fortunate, they are encouraged to talk about how they feel, and they learn to respond to feelings in others. But even the best-intentioned parents and teachers can unwittingly promote coping strategies that get in the way in later life.

To take just a few examples, living with dominant personalities in early life can stop you from standing up for yourself as an adult. A child whose parents had very high expectations may grow up thinking they won't be good enough for the goals they want to reach. Some people avoid leadership responsibility because of a deep need to be liked by everyone. If blowing your own trumpet was always frowned on, you may have an aversion to talking about your strengths. Early setbacks can make some people anxious and risk-averse.

How best do you manage your sense of reluctance? Negative emotions tend to have more of a hold over you than positive ones, so how can you stop unhelpful emotions from running your life? How can you 'unlearn' some of the coping strategies that are no longer working for you? The good news is that the brain is infinitely plastic. With conscious effort, you can train it to be more helpful, but old habits die hard, and you will need the determination to persevere.

Different strategies work for different people. The key message is that you do not have to allow your emotions to hijack you. If you want things to be different, you can choose to take control, and give your rational brain the chance to get involved.

One of the best ways to trump an unhelpful, emotional reaction is to use a different part of your brain – the part that lays down automatic responses to a whole range of situations you have met before. This part of the brain is known to react to events even faster than the emotional part. If you learned some years ago to ride a bike, or drive a car, or use an escalator, you may remember how unfamiliar it felt – yet you now do all of these things without consciously thinking through the movements.

We carry on growing new automatic responses throughout our adult lives. Just think about when you have changed jobs or moved house. For the first few days you may have found yourself heading towards your old route to work or home, but gradually the new route got embedded in your brain and after a while you no longer had to think about it. In the same way, you can teach yourself new responses to stressful situations. You can choose whether to let others' bad behaviour get to you. You can teach yourself to think, and believe, statements like: 'nobody is perfect', 'you can't expect everyone to like you', 'setbacks are valuable learning'.

You can also think about changing your automatic body language. If you are under pressure in a meeting, do you find yourself speaking faster and faster, just because you want to get it over with? Automatically adopting a measured and possibly lower tone can help you feel calmer and is also more likely to hold the attention of your listeners.

Perhaps the most important automatic response is the one that notices your emotional brain is about to cause you a problem. The critical thing is to buy time for your rational brain to catch up. Sometimes all it takes is an automatic (and preferably silent) deep breath. This is of course easier when you are dealing with an email or a text. Yet even when you are face to face with someone you can buy time by allowing a brief silence, or asking a question. While you are doing that, you can try techniques like:

- Asking yourself what you would do if you knew others believed in you – and then acting that way anyway.
- Asking yourself what an admired colleague would do, and acting like them.
- Concentrating on what it would be helpful for the other person to hear from you, rather than having an argument with your inner critic.
- Telling yourself that someone's hostile behaviour could stem from bad news they have just had, or a difficult meeting. Their behaviour is probably nothing to do with you.

It is worth remembering that most of us feel reluctant and inadequate when we are tired. This is because our rational brains run out of energy easily, and our emotional brains take over. We can then be like the hamster on the wheel – running faster and getting nowhere. It pays to give your thinking brain a rest, or switch to some physical or creative activity. Your subconscious will work away in the meantime, and there is a fair chance that you will see a way through when you return to the challenge. We talk about sleeping on a problem for a good reason – it works because it gives your subconscious brain time to do its job.

You may be reluctant to lead because of the leaders you know. You may think they are much better at leading than you – or possibly you may not want to be like them. Understanding your brain may help you to look at them in a different way. They may have the same basic skillset as you, but a different set of emotional responses which have helped them to be successful. If you would like to be more like them, you can study what they do and try it for yourself. For all you know, they may have been on the same journey as you, just a few years ago.

If you don't like the way they lead, that should not stop you aspiring to lead differently. Be honest with yourself about the difference you could make and be ready to promote your ideas. Study the people that you will need to influence, and what is important to them. They will need to know about your achievements, but they will also make some instant emotional judgements. You will want to prompt positive emotions, such as, 'I could trust and respect this person as a colleague', 'this person carries authority without being arrogant', and 'I could be excited by their vision and I believe they could deliver it.'

For reflection

- Does your reluctance stem from deep-rooted beliefs about yourself?
- Do you know what might be triggering your reluctance?
- Try writing about your feelings, or talking about them to someone you trust. Do they still sound convincing?
- Which thinking habits would you like to let go of, and what strategies could help you?
- Ask yourself what you would do if you were not afraid. Does your fear stand up to scrutiny?

PART TWO

Take the plunge

This section is for readers who are hesitant about leadership, or know others who are reluctant to take the plunge.

Building on the discussion about the way our brains work, it explores how we can hold a distorted picture of our strengths and weaknesses. It talks about the fears and assumptions that can prevent us achieving our leadership potential. It suggests some tools and techniques for managing our emotions, challenging our thinking and looking at ourselves in a different light. It ends with tips for building personal resilience, wherever your leadership journey may take you.

3

View yourself objectively

Mike had been working for some years as the psychologist in the HR department of a global company. He advised on recruitment decisions at all levels, from new graduates to members of the Executive Leadership Team, and was greatly respected for his assessments of internal talent. An obvious next career step was to become Head of Talent Recruitment and Development. When the job became vacant, he had no plans to apply. When his wife Sasha, asked him why, he said no one in the company had suggested it to him, and there were others in the department who were bound to be seen as better candidates. The job included team leadership responsibilities, and so far he had worked without any supporting staff.

Sasha was amused to hear this because Mike had so often talked about talented staff – normally women – who would not risk going for a promotion until they were a one hundred per cent fit. She challenged Mike to take some of his own advice and ask himself, 'why not me?'

Some people target more senior roles when they are evidently not ready. Equally, there are many people who have everything it takes, except for self-belief. Such people have a distorted view of themselves. They tend to ignore their strengths and give disproportionate weight to their development needs. If others praise them, they tell themselves it will only be a matter of time before their weaknesses are discovered. If others do not encourage them, they are convinced it is because they are not good enough to get that sort of attention.

Sasha's challenge prompted Mike to ask a trusted colleague, Khaled, to help him with a dispassionate self-assessment. Khaled asked him to write down his strengths, avoiding false modesty. Mike's first attempt was all about his professional expertise in assessing personalities and potential. He needed prompting from Khaled to think about his other skills.

Mike's other skills included his ability to build relationships with people at all levels across the company, his knowledge of the international reach of the company's business and his external networks in recruitment and talent management. Mike also recognized that he was accepted by top management as a trusted advisor, and could always expect his views to be heard with respect. Mike had to admit it all looked quite impressive when written down.

Khaled asked Mike what held him back. He described his lack of line management experience, but he recognized that he had led enough projects across and outside the department to show that he could take people with him, and hold them to account for delivery. He said he could not imagine becoming boss to his current peers – but accepted he had seen plenty of colleagues address that challenge sensitively and successfully.

Finally Mike fell back on the argument that he was not being encouraged by his seniors to apply, so that must mean they did not think him suitable. Khaled asked him whether anyone knew he could be interested in moving out of his specialist role? Mike had to admit he had never talked about it.

Even if you do not have a mentor to talk to, the act of writing down your strengths can help you view yourself more objectively. If you are thinking of applying for a particular role, you can then ask yourself how you would view those strengths if you were the recruiter. Of course you are unlikely to be the perfect fit – but that will be true for most other candidates. The recruiters will be looking for the person who is as close as possible to what they want – and who demonstrates the ability to grow into the areas which are new to them.

The next step is to review the pros and cons of pitching for a role. It can help to write these down in two lists, side by side, and to include any personal factors, like location or working hours. If you are naturally inclined to give more weight to the negative factors, try asking yourself what it would take to shift a few of them into the positives column – for example, if everything else favours your application but the daily commute looks too demanding, might you be able to negotiate to work from home once or twice a week, as an increasing number of people now do?

If you are worried about your lack of line management experience in your job, have you managed people in other roles in your life, such as a volunteer or as a sports captain, and can you demonstrate what skills you have learned from that?

If there is something in the negative column which really is a showstopper, that may mean that you do not apply for the role that is currently available. But the exercise may still be worthwhile if it highlights what you want to work on, to make yourself a stronger contender next time.

It can be worth asking yourself how you would feel if you do not apply and the job is secured by someone you consider to be less well-qualified than you. How will you feel if you see them growing and learning in the role in the way that you could have done? Will you be thankful that it is not you, or will you kick yourself?

In Mike's case, he was persuaded by Khaled and Sasha that he should have a go at applying for the role – but his reluctance did not entirely disappear. He dreaded the thought of having to 'sell himself' in an application and at interview, even though he knew from the other side of the table that this was what was needed. Talking about his strengths and achievements felt too much like boasting. Talking about his vision for the role felt like criticism of his departing boss, who had been very supportive to him.

Mike pictured himself as an outsider offering advice. He knew he would say to someone in his position that recruiters cannot be expected to know instinctively whether you have got what they want. You have to paint the picture for them, so they can imagine you in the role. That means finding out beforehand what really matters to them, and matching your best evidence of past performance to what they need. Then you have to practise describing those past achievements in a concise and compelling way which catches their attention and leaves them wanting to know more.

If this still feels too much like boasting, you can call on third-party endorsement, such as evidence from a 360-degree feedback exercise, praise from stakeholders, or consistently high performance appraisals. This is not the moment for false modesty, as recruiters will make judgements on what they hear and then move on to the next candidate.

Mike was comfortable with his advice to himself, provided he could create plenty of time to rehearse his compelling stories. He realized he could talk about his areas for development in a positive way that showed self-awareness and a determination to learn from watching others and drawing on his wider experience outside work. He could refer with appreciation to everything he had learned from his departing boss, whilst still having ideas of his own on how he would take her legacy forward.

Mike's reluctance to imagine himself as Head of Talent was gradually turning into a desire to learn from the experience of applying. He might even be the strongest candidate.

For reflection

- If you are reluctant to go for a leadership role, are you undervaluing your strengths and exaggerating your development needs?
- Are you honest with yourself about what is holding you back?
- What have you got to lose by pitching for the role? Does a negative assessment stand up to scrutiny?
- Have you practised talking with pride (but not arrogance) about your achievements, and telling the stories in a concise and compelling way?

4

Step into the unknown

The world is full of people who look up at those above them in a hierarchy and think: 'I could never do that.' (It is equally full of people who have no problem imagining themselves in the top jobs, but they are not the focus of this book.)

For some of us, it is hard to imagine doing something that we have not experienced before. We see the demands placed on a leader and we do not know what the toolkit looks like. It feels far safer to stick with the job we know, even if that job is beginning to feel a little too easy. Opportunities are allowed to pass by, until there comes a time when they are no longer offered.

As coaches, we often find ourselves talking to people who are a bit frustrated with their current level of responsibility, yet fearful of stepping into the unknown. Usually they have already progressed their careers beyond the level at which they started, so the first thing we may suggest is to take themselves back to how they felt when they applied for or were offered their current role. Did it feel daunting at the time? What happened to make it less daunting and become more familiar? Can they remember the moment when they felt confident, and why?

Some people say that confidence grew with knowledge of the detailed subject matter. Others talk about the moment when they realized they had the respect of their colleagues and that their opinion was valued. They then begin to analyse how that process came about and to ask why it should not happen again at the next level.

One sticking point can be the assumption that leaders need to know everything of importance at their own level, whilst staying up to date with all the detail that they knew when they were more junior. Clearly there comes a time when that approach is unsustainable – and observation of any successful senior person will show them trusting others to take care of the detail for them. It is a tall order to ask anyone to let go of the things that make them feel most competent, in order to start learning all over again. Yet it can also be immensely satisfying to coach others to do the things you now find easy, and to seek to learn from people who have gone ahead of you and scaled the next mountain.

Another mental block can be a sense of inferiority, compared to others at the next level. People report feeling intimidated at meetings of their seniors, and afraid to speak – even when they know they have something valuable to say. We ask them whether those meetings feel any different if they are there on behalf of their boss, and imbued with that person's authority. They nearly always say yes, it does feel different if they are there on behalf of their boss and feel their views are being heard with respect. We encourage them to go to more meetings imagining they are representing the boss. The more they can act the part, the more they will feel accepted by others, and the less daunting it will seem. Remember that all these other people had to step into the unknown themselves a few years ago.

Doing something outside of your comfort zone can bring fresh energy into your life at work. Imagine yourself in ten or 20 years' time, still in the same job. Would you feel content, or would you wish you had found the confidence to aim higher?

Maria's story is an example of someone reluctant to step into the unknown. Her boss called her into his office one morning to tell her that he was about to resign. Maria was sad to hear he was going, and alarmed when he said he would be expected to leave immediately, since he was joining a competitor. Someone would need to act up in his place until a successor could be recruited, and Maria was the obvious choice.

Maria's boss said he would talk to her later after he had spoken to their Head of Department, and she spent the rest of the day trying to think of alternatives to his idea. It terrified Maria to think she might have to fill his shoes for weeks, even months – and how would the rest of her work get done?

Later in the day, they had another conversation. Her boss said that their Head of Department had every confidence in Maria's ability to stand in, and would be offering her temporary promotion. Maria thanked him, then told him how worried she felt. He reminded Maria that she had deputized successfully for him in the past. The difference this time was that it would be for a longer period, so Maria would need to free up her time from her current job. He talked her through the options, and reminded her there would be some flexibility in the salary budget once he was gone.

Maria realized she could temporarily promote Guy, her most capable team member, to fill her job, and backfill behind Guy with an agency temp. Guy was keen to advance his career and already knew a lot of her job: he would just need counselling from her on how to get the best from some key relationships. By the end of the day, Maria realized that the real challenge was to get herself into a different mindset, and to see this turn of events as an opportunity to find out whether senior leadership appealed.

For reflection

- If you study a role at the next level, can you pinpoint what you would need to do differently, compared to your present job?

- Remember progress is as much about relationships and influence as it will be about understanding the subject matter.

- What opportunities can you take now to practise some of those wider level skills – for example by offering to stand in for your boss?

- Remind yourself that your team members need you to delegate and grow in confidence, so that they can themselves step up when the time comes.

5

Find your vocation

Julie had been head of a department in a secondary school for a number of years and loved the interaction with young people. She got a lot of satisfaction through seeing their growth in academic understanding and their development into adulthood. A number of Julie's students came from tough backgrounds. Julie had the knack of catching their imagination and enabling them to stretch their expectations. She helped turn grumpy fourteen year olds into engaged and positive sixteen year olds.

Her friends observed Julie as an effective and capable teacher and leader of other teachers, but Julie was not sure that her long-term vocation was to be in a secondary school. Julie felt even more fulfilled in her contribution at her local church where she had a developing role working with students. Julie felt at home in the church community interacting with people of all ages from children to the elderly.

A couple of friends suggested to Julie that she would be a capable church leader: she brought the humility necessary to be a good priest, alongside an ability to engage with a range of different people.

Julie felt an initial reluctance to explore this possibility but she trusted the wisdom of these friends. Gradually she felt a sense of vocation or calling to explore ordination into the Anglican priesthood. Some of her colleagues at the school were surprised; others saw such a move as a natural progression. Others recognized the strong sense of calling in Julie and were very supportive of her.

Doing the training was hard work as Julie was combining it with her full-time teaching role. What kept her going was the ever-growing sense of vocation to ordained ministry and church leadership. She hoped one day to be the vicar in a parish that included a significant number of students. That would be fulfilment for her, while recognizing that there were many uncertainties about her future steps.

A sense of vocation is stronger for some than others. Many doctors will say that the desire to be qualified as a doctor originated in their teenage years. A sense of vocation has led many people to work in overseas aid or to seek roles in health or caring charities.

For some, going into politics either locally or nationally is a response to a desire to make a significant difference in society. It is only because of that sense of vocation that individuals find they can live through the criticism they often experience if they enter political life.

For some people the language of vocation or calling is important. The appropriate language for some is about making a difference to other people's lives. For others the language might be about finding a higher purpose that is relevant for you. Believing you have a calling or vocation can give you a strength of commitment and resolve that will take you through difficult times.

The risk of believing you have a strong sense of vocation or calling is that you can become too single-minded for your own good. There is a risk of becoming blinkered, with a limited willingness to be adaptable in the light of changing circumstances. Hence the importance of being able to talk through with trusted others how your sense of vocation or calling is developing and whether it passes the tests of both realism and aspiration.

For other people the language of vocation or calling is not relevant. You may well see your primary responsibility in life being as a parent. Work is a necessary means of raising funds to fulfil your family responsibilities. Work is functional rather than aspirational. If this is your starting point it is still worth exploring what in your work gives you fulfilment and where you want to make a significant contribution that will benefit others. You may be employed in banking because it pays well: but can you also see your role as enabling financial markets to work effectively to the benefit of economic communities and human societies?

You might be a technician because you enjoyed training as a technician. But how might those technical skills develop into something beyond making a technical contribution yourself? Perhaps there might be a growing aspiration to develop the skills of apprentices. It might appeal to join some groups of like-minded people who are looking creatively at ways of getting tasks done faster and more effectively.

Whatever you do, it is worth asking how you could help make the lives of other people more interesting and fulfilled. The calling of the builder is to construct houses that will last. The calling of the architect may be to design buildings that lead to good quality interaction amongst staff and clients.

Sometimes following your vocation can feel like very hard work. There are always going to be tough times when you question whether your calling to be a teacher, priest, doctor or technician is sustainable. At these moments it is important to remember why you entered a particular world and what has sustained you so far.

Keeping in your mind's eye the positive comments from others from the past helps sustain you for the future. Sometimes in the desert moment you have to hold on to the belief that your vocation is right for you. When the desert moments pass you will be stronger and more self-reliant than before.

Julie found working as a curate tough. She had been used to running her own department at the secondary school with adequate resources and staff who were under her leadership. As a curate she was working for a vicar who had a very different approach to leadership. She was working with volunteers in the church and not paid staff: hence she could not plan in the same, precise way that she had been used to as a school head of department. There were moments when Julie questioned her vocation and had to return in her thinking to why she had made this choice, but there was encouragement too, often in unexpected ways.

After four years Julie was appointed as incumbent of an inner-city church with a diverse congregation, including a number of students. Julie was conscious of the weight of responsibility on her. She was effectively chief executive of a small organization with an uncertain financial base. What kept her going was the variety of work, the range of people she was dealing with, the flexibility in her use of time and her sense of vocation that she was helping to make a difference in people's lives.

It was hard going. She had much shorter holidays than when she was a schoolteacher. The expectations on her were seven days a week. There was a never-ending list of jobs to be done. There was a fickleness in the commitment and contribution of the people at the church, but Julie was comfortable in herself that she had made the right decision to follow her sense of calling. She felt fulfilled and blessed, if often exhausted. Julie was grateful that she had overcome her initial reluctance to be ordained as a priest and had moved into church leadership.

For reflection

- To what extent do you feel a sense of vocation or calling?
- How might you explore where a sense of vocation or calling might take you?
- Is there something holding you back from following a sense of vocation or calling?

6

Confront your fear of failure

Sam felt that his reputation was on the line every day. He was waiting for others to spot his weaknesses. If a senior colleague was abrupt with him, he would worry that he had said something they thought stupid, or that he had explained himself badly. Sometimes he would lie awake at night going over a conversation and imagining the worst possible consequences. Even though he was seen as one of the best performers at his level, Sam could not imagine going for a bigger role. The fear of failure was too great.

It is not unusual to meet people like Sam, because it is often the high achievers who worry most about failure. They may have had stellar track records at school and in higher education – yet have worried dreadfully before each exam hurdle that this time their weaknesses would be found out. One mistake in answering a question would lead to a firm conviction that they had messed up completely, and many anxious weeks before the results came out. It would not help that friends and family thought the anxiety was overdone. Unless something happened to break the pattern, this anxiety would often follow them into the world of work, and sometimes affect their capacity for happiness in their personal life.

There are plenty of theories on what causes this sort of mindset. Stanford psychologist Carol Dweck concluded from 20 years of research with children and adults that many high achievers value their reputation for being 'clever' or 'smart' above everything else. She talks about every situation requiring the person to prove themselves, because the consequences of not doing so feel too awful. Meanwhile, others around them see failure simply as a learning opportunity.

Further insights come from Eric Berne's work on the 'lifescripts' we tend to write for ourselves as children, and live out in adulthood without realizing. We tend to distort our perception of reality to fit the lifescript, and to discount evidence that does not fit. Some adults have acquired particularly strong lifescripts that tell them it is essential to please the important people in their lives. Everything they do must be perfect, or they will disappoint others and themselves.

It is surprising how often a client mentions that their parents' approval was very important to them but not easily won. Stories such as 'how come you were only second in that race?' or 'you normally get straight As, so you must have been slacking', can have a profound effect if regularly repeated. The parent's disappointment becomes the doubting voice in the adult's ear that says 'you are not good enough'.

Early setbacks can make some people more resilient, but others can become anxious and risk-averse. The voice in their head says: 'this situation feels like the last time that everything went wrong', even if the circumstances are quite different.

Sometimes, it can be enough for someone like Sam to know that he is far from alone in his feelings. Just talking about them can help bring things into perspective. However, for most people, these are deep-seated ways of thinking that will not disappear without practice. There are some exercises which can help to retrain the brain. They involve writing things down, simply because that can bring greater clarity than when you try to hold ideas in your head.

One approach is to divide a page into two columns. In the first column you list all the triggers you can think of which cause self-doubt and a drop in confidence. In the second column, you list the strategies which have helped you into a more positive frame of mind. An example in Sam's case might be that he feels a fool when he has made a comment he thinks is stupid. In the right-hand column he might find himself writing things like: 'for all I know, the other person didn't think the comment was stupid. If they did, they have far more pressing things on their mind to worry about it. Anyway, my credibility is high with them, and one comment is not going to undermine it.'

Taking this further, you could ask yourself what or who helped you in the past to banish a sense of inadequacy, and could you mobilize that support again when needed? That help can take different forms for different personality types. For some, it comes from knowing how much others value them and seek their company. For others, what helps is some reflection time on their own, or a burst of exercise, to get life in perspective. For many, it is about giving their brains a rest from work problems, knowing they will operate better when they return to those problems refreshed. In Sam's case, he knew that lying awake at night was not helping his daytime energies, and recognized that he always slept better if he stopped looking at emails at least an hour before going to bed.

You might ask yourself the question: 'what would I do if I was not afraid?' This means forcing yourself to write down or say out loud what you are afraid of, and then examine the likelihood of the feared event materializing. Even if it happened, how serious would that be?

These techniques can be helpful when you have some reflection time, but you also need strategies for dealing with self-doubt at the moment it surfaces. Self-doubt is an emotional reaction, and you need to create a breathing space for your rational brain to sense check what the inner critic is saying. This is easier when you are dealing with something in writing, like an email, than it is when you are face to face with someone. Even in a meeting, though, you can allow a short silence before reacting to what feels like someone else attacking you, or you can buy time with a question seeking clarification.

Try observing yourself as if you were a third person, watching from a gallery. Ask yourself as the observer whether your emotional response deserves any attention. Even if it does, is it helpful to you in handling the situation, or is it best to park it till later and focus on the business in hand?

Ask yourself how you would behave if you knew that the other person was supportive of you, and if you discovered you were misinterpreting their facial expression or tone of voice. If that makes you more confident, act that way anyway.

If time and circumstances allow, rehearse your emotions afterwards to someone you trust, or write them down, and then bring some logic to the situation. What would be a more useful way of looking at this?

After some months of discussion and reflection, Sam decided he did not want his fear of failure to run his life. He was not about to become a massive risk-taker but he would start venturing outside his comfort zone. He might even think about applying for promotion. Sam gave his inner critic a name. He thought about it as a parrot sitting on his shoulder and muttering unhelpful thoughts in his ear. He learned to tell it to shut up.

For reflection

- Do others tend to have a much higher opinion of your abilities than you do?
- Is fear of failure making you reluctant to fulfil your potential?
- Can you talk to someone you trust about what you are afraid of, and why? Invite them to press you on whether you are catastrophizing or losing a sense of perspective.
- Try some of the exercises in this chapter. Then ask yourself whether you are choosing to let your fear of failure dictate your future.

7

Have the courage of your convictions

Zara had joined an engineering firm as a new graduate. As her role grew, she found she was good at attracting and keeping talent, and that her team had a strong reputation for delivering results. Her managers were impressed. They also saw in her an answer to the challenge from above that they should be promoting more women into senior roles. Zara was flattered, but found she was reluctant to put herself forward. She had no doubt that she was capable of doing senior roles, but felt strongly that she did not fit the firm's leadership culture. She did not want to feel pressurized into being something she was not.

Zara's dilemma is a familiar one, and it is not confined to women. We often talk to men who look upwards and feel they do not share the values of their leaders. That is not to say who is right or wrong – it is simply a reflection of the culture that has developed in the organization in the preceding years. Sometimes the answer is to accept that this is not the place to advance your career – but what if you love what you do and know that this culture may be typical of the sector? What if you get a clear message from your team that they would like to see more people like you at the top?

Before doing anything else, be absolutely clear with yourself about the values you hold, and why. Write them down, or talk to others about them. Could you explain how wider adoption of these values could help the organization to be more successful?

To put it bluntly, you are much more likely to get a hearing from above, if you can show there is something in it for them.

A key question is whether you want to be one of the pioneers who seeks to break the mould. Each individual will answer this question differently, depending on their circumstances, but it can help to have a framework for reaching a conclusion. A useful starting point is to study a few people like you who have made it against the odds in similar organizations, and to find out what worked for them. Our observation is that there are some recurring themes.

Such people tend to be realistic about what they can hope to change in the culture whilst moving up – as opposed to what they might be able to change when they get there. They identify their levers by imagining themselves in the shoes of the senior leaders and working out what is likely to be on their minds. They aim to find out what the senior leaders really care about and want to be known for. If they do not know, they try working through the 'gatekeepers' who spend a lot of time with the top team, such as the PAs, the Board Secretary, or the person who supports the top team on their internal communications. For example, they explore whether the firm is under external pressure from shareholders or regulators to show that it is changing some practices. Are there internal worries about loss of expensively trained talent? Are there persistent concerns surfacing in staff opinion surveys?

Once someone who is determined to be a change agent has identified the levers, they raise their profile as someone who can help with solutions to such problems. You can adopt a similar approach. You can show how your team has solved problems by adopting the values you are promoting. You might join organization-wide committees or task forces that are looking at current management concerns, and volunteer to lead or join the presentation to the top team. If this approach feels calculated, see it as an intellectual challenge to work out what or who influences shifts in culture. Organizational politics are a fact of life, wherever you work.

Another theme for successful mould-breakers is about allies and support networks. You need them for both practical and emotional reasons. You need to find out who else would be willing to work on the levers with you, and which senior colleagues are most likely to be supportive. In emotional terms, you need to know who believes in you and will be there for you when the going gets tough.

Support can come from outside the organization as much as from inside – there are family and friends, but you might also know someone who is prepared to be an external mentor. They need not necessarily be working in the same world as you: what matters is that they can empathize with what you are trying to achieve, and have had experience of tackling similar cultural challenges.

It can feel hard to stay true to yourself when you come up against behaviours you do not admire. It feels unnatural and stressful to imitate those behaviours, and the more unnatural it feels, the more likely you are to attract labels such as 'defensive' or 'aggressive'. In many organizations, there is a fine line for middle managers to walk, between being seen as not assertive enough and over-assertive. If you are not assertive enough, you can easily be ignored, but if you are seen as over-assertive, even disrespectful, you are not influential either. Such assessments can feel unfair, but if you look at any society, including in the animal kingdom, you will see the same thing happening. The best response is normally to build one to one relationships through learning about individuals and their personalities, and working out what brings out the best and worst in them.

Once you have earned trust and respect, do not be too thrown out if others sometimes behave unhelpfully, even aggressively, in a group discussion. If you do find yourself on the receiving end of sharp words in a group meeting, it may be nothing to do with you: it could equally reflect conflict within the top team over an earlier agenda item, or competition to impress the leader.

The key is to know who you are and what matters to you and then to choose when you need to vary your style deliberately to achieve a purpose. That should feel quite different from trying to bend yourself out of shape to be something you are not. You stay in control – and you can discard the props when you no longer need them. The difference that you bring becomes a positive benefit that your colleagues would not want to lose.

Zara decided to put aside any thoughts of promotion whilst she explored the firm's openness to change. She knew many talented middle managers who were frustrated by a rather paternalistic approach at the top. The leadership team had all known each other for many years, socialized together, and genuinely believed that they had the firm's best interests at heart. She learned through chatting to the Board Secretary that the top team were increasingly worried about the high resignation rate of managers in their 30s and the risk this represented to their legacy.

When Zara heard that consultants were to be called in, she spotted her opportunity. She volunteered to join the staff group which was to work with the consultants, and offered her team as a case study of an area with low resignation rates. The consultants explored the differences between her team and other areas, and fed their conclusions into their report to the Board. It emerged that delegation and empowerment were critical motivators, as was the recognition that middle managers with young families valued flexible working practices. Zara accepted that the culture was not going to change overnight, but a conversation had started, and she began to feel she could be a part of the future.

For reflection

- Are you holding back from realizing your potential, because you look upwards and cannot identify with the culture you see?

- Are you convinced that a shift in culture would help your organization to be more successful?

- Which would you rather do: walk away, or have a go at influencing the culture for the better?

8

Do not be afraid of interviews and assessment

Some people are not at all reluctant about taking a leadership position. They are confident that they know what they would do and how they would do it. The problem is they cannot face the assessment process which would get them there. Often they have had a humiliating experience at an interview in the past, and the thought of going through that again fills them with dread. So they stay in their current job, feeling increasingly frustrated that they are not getting the chance to apply their learning on a bigger stage. Their frustration is made worse if their seniors tell them they would make a good leader – but still require them to go through the selection process.

No selection process is perfect, but most organizations agree that an open competition is a fairer way of choosing leaders than an informal 'tap on the shoulder'. The evidence suggests that all sorts of unconscious bias can creep in, and can lead to legal challenge. Fighting against the process is not going to help. This chapter is about how you can make it less of an ordeal – and manage the negative emotions from any previous bad experience.

As always, it pays to imagine yourself in other people's shoes. If you were applying for the job you want to fill, what would matter most to you and how would you look for evidence? The criteria in the job advert ought to give you some insight, but so will stories being told in the organization, or commentary by outsiders, including the media. Do your research. Then you need to develop concise and compelling stories which illustrate that you have the qualities and experience the recruiters are looking for. You can weave some of these examples into the job application, and you should have a bank of them ready for use at interview.

So far, so good, but if you hate the thought of interviews, you still have to get over your stage fright. There are techniques for this, if you are ready to work at it. It starts with rehearsing your stories until you are totally comfortable with using them. Of course you do not know which questions will be asked, nor in which order, so in this respect it will not be like learning a script – but the more the stories are embedded in your brain, the easier it will be to recall them when you need them, and the less you will worry about drying up.

If it helps to have a structure to your stories, try the STAR approach:

- Summarize in a sentence the SITUATION you were facing.
- Describe briefly how you defined the TASK.
- Explain the ACTION you took – in a few key bullet points.
- Finish with the RESULT you achieved.

Each story should not take more than one minute to tell. Try rehearsing your examples out loud, so you know what they sound like. Ideally you will find someone to listen as if they were an interviewer, and give you feedback on how you come across. If that is not possible, video your efforts and force yourself to play them back, or observe yourself in a mirror.

Assume that you will not like your first attempts. You probably won't have made your points sharply enough, or in the most convincing order. You may have taken too long to get to the point of your answer – or not have got there at all. Don't despair. That is the reason for practising. The more you rehearse and get feedback, the better you will be, and the more natural it will feel.

The next thing is to remember that your interviewers are human beings and thus incapable of being totally objective (however hard they try). The facts of your career history are important to them, but they will almost certainly be influenced, too, by the personal impression you make.

If you know who is going to be on the panel, find out what you can about their background, personality and interests. Then you can avoid using an example which a panel member might interpret as critical of everything they stand for, and hopefully choose examples which will ring positive bells with them. If you have discovered that a panel member has a reputation for being provocative, you need not be thrown when they challenge everything you say. It may be their way of testing your resilience.

If you are pitching for a leadership role, the selectors will look for signs that you can engage them as equals, build influential relationships and carry teams with you. Look at them when you speak – not at the table. Show that you are listening to them and building on what they say. Don't talk too fast or get caught up in long, complicated narratives.

Above all, let your natural warmth come through, and remember to smile periodically. You need to look as though you would love to do the job, and not that you are desperate to get out of the room as fast as possible.

You will almost certainly get a question you have not prepared for. Do not be afraid to leave a short silence whilst you think of an answer. It is better to stop and think than plunge into an answer that you know you cannot defend. If you can't bear a silence, try playing back the question as though you are checking you have understood correctly. Just saying it out loud may release your thinking capacity.

If you still cannot find the perfect answer, don't dwell on it and let it influence the rest of the interview. Tell yourself that one weak answer is unlikely to count for much if you have handled everything else well.

Remember to act and dress for the role that you want. The degree of formality will depend on the world you work in, but if in doubt, dress up rather than down. Selection panels are often influenced more than they would admit by whether they consider a candidate to be 'smart' or 'well-groomed'. Most of us feel and act more self-confident when we feel good about how we look.

If you prepare and practise thoroughly, the interview will feel more familiar when it happens, which in itself should help to dampen down the bad memories of a previous occasion. But if you need some more tools to calm your nerves, tell yourself that everything in life happens for a reason, and maybe you needed that earlier setback to learn from. The circumstances are different now. You are older and more experienced, and you are ready to give the performance of your life.

Alex was well known in the health charity world for his success as a fundraiser. He was always full of creative ideas, and excellent at building relationships with major donors. One morning he had a call from headhunters looking for a Director of Fundraising. It was a job he would love, in an organization he really admired. Yet he hesitated.

A year previously, he had applied for the Director role in his own organization and sailed through to the interview stage, then fallen on his face. He still smarted from the memory of his inability to address the questions, his rambling attempts at answers, and his rising sense of panic as the panel put him under pressure.

Luckily for him, Alex had a friend who asked him whether he was always going to let that bad experience hold him back, and probed whether he could have approached that interview differently. Talking it through, he realized he had been over-complacent in thinking that he knew the organization, and the selection panel, and had walked into the interview thinking he could improvise and charm his way through. Rigorous preparation was not in his nature, but here was an occasion where he had to do it, or forever remain at his current level.

For reflection

- Are you reluctant to apply for a leadership role you would love for fear of the selection process?
- Do you know what you are afraid of?
- Could you reduce your fears by thorough preparation?
- If this is about stage fright or exam nerves, have you explored the techniques that could help you?

9

Reframe the challenge

Rhiannon felt vaguely dissatisfied in her administrative job in a small further education college. She liked her colleagues and enjoyed being around young people who were older than her own primary-aged daughter, but she felt her strengths were not being fully used. She had an accountancy qualification, and before her daughter was born, she had been in charge of operations at a busy housing association. She could easily see how the college and its suppliers could be run more efficiently and effectively.

A friend on the staff reminded her that the Bursar was due to retire at the end of the college year. Rhiannon's instant reaction of 'I could do that' was followed by 'but not yet'. She quickly dismissed the idea as impracticable.

It can be very frustrating when you know you have leadership strengths, but feel circumstances won't let you use them. Many people with carer responsibilities decide they must put their career on hold, and we would never argue with that. We would only encourage the Rhiannons of this world to analyse the issue first, and check if there is a way to reconcile their priorities. By reframing the challenge, you may be able to find a way forward.

To free up your brain, write your thinking down, or talk to someone who will listen, and will ask questions, but will not impose their own solution. You could try an exercise like listing all the reasons that work against you going for the role and all those which work in favour. The next step might be to ask yourself what could possibly happen to reduce the reasons against, and strengthen the reasons in favour. Take a brainstorming approach and leave the critique till later. When, and only when, all of your ideas are on the chart, you should ask yourself what would need to happen to make some of these ideas feasible. How much do you want to make the shift? Is there anyone you could enlist in your support?

Another approach can be to put yourself in the shoes of the recruiters for the post. What skills and experience do they need for the organization to be successful? How much do they need someone like you and how likely are they to find what they want in the current market? If you were them, what compromises might you be prepared to make to get the ideal candidate?

The aim is to view your choices from a different perspective. Someone in Rhiannon's situation might notice that her reasons for ruling herself out were based on assumptions that were worth testing. Employers are required to consider whether jobs can be done in reduced or flexible hours, and are often willing to compromise in order to get the best candidate. Increasingly, they are open to the idea of job-shares between two suitably qualified candidates who can demonstrate how they will work together. There is no need to assume they want the job done the way it has always been done.

The other assumptions to explore are more personal. They are often grounded in our desire to do the best for our families, and for others who may depend on us for support. Every individual finds their own way forward, but it is worth checking every so often whether we have boxed ourselves in unnecessarily.

The parent who assumes that their child always wants to be

picked up from school by them, and them alone, may overlook the fact that the child would be happy to go to an after school club once a week, or walk home occasionally to a friend's house. The son or daughter who feels tied to visiting an elderly parent each day may have become so entrenched in the routine that they do not stand back and explore who else might be able to help – or indeed what their parent might prefer.

Rhiannon's reasons for wanting the Bursar's role were that she knew she could do it and do it well. She also recognized that the Principal would have a hard time finding someone with her skills and experience, and knowledge of the college, who was prepared to do the job on the salary offered.

Gradually, and after talking to her parents and husband, a possible approach emerged. Rhiannon believed she could do the job in her current hours because she was more productive in her use of time than the current Bursar. If the Principal was nervous about that, Rhiannon's own replacement could be recruited to work longer hours. Rhiannon's parents said they would do the school run if something urgent came up which genuinely required her to stay later at work. If there was a backlog of tasks at the end of the week, her husband was ready to take their daughter swimming for a couple of hours, whilst Rhiannon caught up using the laptop that the school could give her. Indeed her husband said he would enjoy the swimming trip, as he commuted during the week and rarely had one to one time with their little girl.

Rhiannon had a possible solution – but only she could decide whether she now wanted to talk to the Principal about it, and think about making an application.

For reflection

- Could your reluctance to go for a leadership role be linked to assumptions which are worth challenging?

- Are you ready to examine those assumptions critically and ask whether they are serving you well?

- Let your creativity loose for a moment, and talk to others who could be helpful to you. Would the consequences of letting go of your assumptions be as serious as you have allowed yourself to think?

- Is there a way forward which could work for everyone?

10

Know your sources of support

Reluctance to pitch for leadership can sometimes be based on apprehension about a new location and/or a change from a familiar employer to an unknown quantity. You may have been offered a leadership post in a new country, or at a UK location far from family and friends. The challenge can be especially acute if you are moving on your own or have to be separated from a partner or children during the week.

There may be good reasons for turning down the leadership opportunity, but it is worth letting your rational brain explore the pros and cons first, and writing them down. Then you can ask yourself whether the exercise changes the way you feel.

Matt was divorced, with no children. He worked for a company which managed marinas in the UK. The firm wanted him to head up a new venture in Hong Kong, and thought he was the perfect choice because he had no ties, and no children whose education would have to be funded. The firm assumed Matt would jump at the chance but he said he needed time to think about it. Matt was not someone to make friends easily and it had taken him some while to build a network through his local sailing club, where people had been very supportive after his marriage ended. He was close to his brother and family and his mother, who remained sources of emotional support when he was feeling low.

Matt had heard that expatriate life in Hong Kong valued people who worked hard and played hard – and that play was more linked to the late-night bars than the outdoor life he loved. On the other hand, this could be a great opportunity to 'run his own show', and the initial commitment was only for two years. The pay was good, and the taxes low. He should be able to afford a house of his own in the UK at the end of the two years, especially if he was prepared to travel to work from a less expensive housing area.

Relocating is a big decision, even when you are taking your family with you, or know people at the new location. Most people will ask their company for time to do some practical research, and then to work through the pros and cons. You will want to talk to someone who knows the location about the cost of living, climate, and quality of life. Matt, for example, might be reassured to know that there is a group of serious runners who enjoy the challenging hiking trails in the New Territories. He would hear that hot sticky summers could be an issue, but that mild winters are a plus. He might want to know about air quality, and where to go to get away from pollution hot spots. He might be pleased to hear that he could get hold of most of his favourite foods.

It is critical that the research covers how to build new support networks, especially when the location is too far away for casual visitors. Skype, Facetime and social media are good ways of staying in touch with family and friends at home, but there is a limit to what a virtual support network can offer. This is the moment for creative thinking about ways of meeting people that will not take you too far out of your comfort zone. Are there networks of professionals at this location who work in a similar field to yours? Are there clubs or societies that match your favourite leisure activities? Could you volunteer at a local charity or church and meet people through helping others? Do you or your friends have any contacts at the location who could introduce you to a few people and help you to get started?

Normally, there will be opportunities to build new relationships at work. This can feel difficult if the role on offer is the most senior job in the organization, and there can be risks in getting too close to work colleagues. But a good leader can draw strength and support from a trusted team of direct reports without losing authority. Think about the best teams you have belonged to, or observed. In high performing teams you will see the leader confidently drawing on the strengths of their direct reports, in the belief that this is more effective than the heroic model.

Having explored the scope for support networks, you might want to think about challenges specific to the job, which will be different from what you are used to. How much change would you be trying to take on in one go? Would it look less daunting if you got some preparation time beforehand and made that a condition of accepting the offer? It would be reasonable to ask, for example, for some cultural acclimatization if you know that business is done very differently from business in your home country. It could be sensible to get some training in advance, if there is going to be more exposure to the press and TV than you have been used to, or a requirement to be more active on social media.

You will want to find out about the key stakeholders and their expectations. If there is someone currently in the post for which you are being recruited, what seems to work well and less well for them in these relationships? What do you need to know about how these players tick? Find out who can give you insights so that forewarned is forearmed.

Finally, you need to anticipate how you will stay resilient when the pressures are on. If you feel trapped in a spiral of anxiety, your brain needs a chance to recharge whilst you stand back and appraise what is happening. Every individual has their own way of relieving stress, but you may not have thought consciously about what works for you. Some people need physical exercise, others divert to a non-work activity which requires their total concentration. The aim is to switch your brain from worrying, and to focus on something completely different. When you return refreshed to your challenges, the odds are that you will see them in a new light.

When he wrote his analysis down, Matt was struck by a couple of things, including the possibility of building a real sense of purpose with the three managers who would report to him as head of the new venture. Two of them were local to Hong Kong and understood both the Chinese and the expatriate business cultures. They were too inexperienced at the moment to head the venture, but both could be credible candidates in two years' time. The other, a Dane, was planning to retire soon, but knew everything there was to know about the marina business, and was a seasoned media performer who was happy to mentor others. Together, the four of them could build something pretty exciting.

Matt went off for a sailing weekend whilst he let his thinking gestate – but he already thought he knew what he was going to say to his boss on Monday.

For reflection

* If you are concerned about relocating to take a leadership role, have you thought about how your support networks operate at the moment, and your chances of replicating them?

* Have you thought about the strength you could draw from your senior team, if you have a sense of common goals?

* Is there specific training that you need in advance? Can you ask for it before you accept the role?

* Do you know what keeps you sane when the going gets tough – and can you make sure it stays part of your life, however much time pressure you are under?

11

Keep a sense of perspective

We all discover on a leadership journey that from every summit you see another one. Even the small number of people who reach the pinnacle of their organization are likely to be asking themselves what everyone thinks of their performance, and whether they should at some stage pitch to be leader of something bigger or more meaningful. It seems appropriate at this transition stage between the two sections of the book to reflect on how we keep a sense of perspective about life and work.

Wherever we are in our career or home life, we all have times when the weight of expectations upon us, or the pressure of events, can feel too much to bear. Different personalities can respond in different ways. Some people drive themselves and others harder and harder, risking exhaustion. Some retreat into ever more detailed analysis of what is happening, in the hope that a magic solution will suddenly appear. Others will vent their sense of unfairness that this should be happening to them, and look for someone to blame. Other people want to curl up and hide, in the hope that someone will come to their rescue.

These reactions are all understandable, but unlikely to help much. The most balanced individuals accept the new reality and remind themselves that they are as capable as anyone of finding a way out of problems. However pressured the situation, this is the moment to stand back and imagine what an impartial, cool-headed observer might say. What are the critical goals in this situation and are you being distracted from them by sideshows or the speed of events? Who are the key stakeholders and what matters most to them? What are the key risks and how can they be managed? How can you keep people refreshed and motivated if this is going to be a long haul?

Identify the colleagues who can help you brainstorm these questions and do not be afraid to ask for their help. Talking things through with others is a sign of strength, provided it is not an excuse to keep delaying decisions.

Ask yourself what the observer might notice about your emotional state. It may be hard to stay cool and logical when you feel that your future could be at stake, but can you force yourself to articulate what is causing you the greatest anxiety? What is the worst thing that could happen in this scenario and how likely is it? We can all have a tendency to catastrophize under stress, which is counterproductive because it prevents us thinking straight. Even if you believe that a problem is your fault, treat that feeling as an incentive to put things right, rather than a reason to beat yourself up.

It is likely that you have survived such periods of pressure in the past, whether in your work or personal life. What did you learn from that earlier time that will help you now? What worked and what would you do differently? Many people look back on an earlier experience and realize they bottled up their feelings too much for fear of seeming weak, or out of a desire not to worry anyone. They recognize that it could have helped to talk to a trusted friend or family member who was completely detached from the problem and its context.

The people you talk with do not need to provide solutions.

Indeed, you may want to specify up front that you would rather they did not offer solutions. All you may need them to do is to listen to you and allow you to formulate your thinking out loud. If your thoughts are too chaotic, they may gently help you with a structure, so that you can begin to see what your options are. They may also remind you that you are not totally defined by your work, and that there are many other aspects of your life which are a source of strength and joy. They may even help you to smile and see the humour in the situation.

An important factor will be your ability to look after yourself. This is not selfish: it is essential. Think about the instruction on an airline flight that you need your own oxygen mask on, before you can help others. This means getting adequate sleep, eating properly and ensuring that your tired brain gets the chance to refresh.

Some people recharge their batteries by meditation and prayerfulness, others by immersing themselves in music or art, enjoying the natural world around them, or playing with children. You need to know what works for you and make time for it, because it will make you more productive. The same goes for the people around you, whose wellbeing is equally important. If you have a marathon to run as a team, you cannot afford to exhaust everyone in the first few days.

Even if the challenge feels never-ending, remind yourself that it, too, will pass. It may feel like the end of the world if you do not achieve everything that is being asked of you, but it won't be. The world will move on. You need only think about the media spotlight on a public figure when a 'story' blows up. At the time, that person will feel as though there is no place to hide, but within a few weeks nearly everyone has forgotten what the story was all about. The challenge for the individual is to put the story behind them too. Check whether there are lessons you need to learn for the future, or any relationships you need to mend, then recognize that dwelling on the past is bad for your mental health. You have survived before and you will survive again.

When you hit a spell of trouble, however painful it feels, ask yourself, 'what is this trying to teach me?' Remind yourself of all the leaders in history who survived difficult setbacks and were the stronger for it. Think about the great sporting heroes who learn from analysing their defeats and focus on what it would take to win next time. Reflect on the mental strength of the Paralympians, whose determination has led to achievements that many could not have believed possible. They are all realistic about what needs to be done, and the work involved. They all also know that a positive attitude greatly increases the chances of success.

For reflection

- Are you prepared to accept the reality of your current situation and work out your future options, or are you preoccupied with wishing things were different?
- Are you aware of your emotional responses when you are under pressure and do you have strategies for managing them?
- Do you pay enough attention to your personal support networks, so that you know where to turn in times of trouble?
- Do you recognize that you have a duty to look after your health and well being, if you are to be of any help to others?

PART THREE

Come out of the shadows

This section is about people already in leadership roles who are finding it hard to think and act the part. It explores some of the reasons which may hold them back. They may not know how to manage the multiple demands of leadership on their time and be reluctant to let go of the expert role that got them promotion. They may be daunted by their new responsibilities and the senior stakeholders they need to influence. They may find it hard to manage their emotional reactions to others, and to handle those people's emotional reactions to them.

These chapters suggest ways to understand why we react as we do to leadership challenges, and tools for taking control. It ends by looking at the coaching role of leaders in enabling others to step up with confidence.

12

Recognize your sources of authority

John relished doing scientific experiments. At school he had excelled in chemistry and physics and got immense satisfaction from his research at university. After doing a Doctorate he moved into a scientific career in an organization which managed complex laboratories. John was good at inspiring people because of his creative thinking and determination to ensure that experiments were thoroughly executed with clear and comprehensive outcomes.

John was ambitious to do well and was a popular choice to lead the work of the laboratory when it was granted significant funds for further research. John was both thrilled by the appointment and taken aback by the volume of work he was now responsible for. He soon realized that he would not be able to devote the time and commitment necessary to lead experiments himself. This harsh reality came as both a shock and a disappointment. After feeling overwhelmed for a couple of weeks John questioned, in his own mind, whether he had made the correct choice in accepting this promotion. He felt he had lost authority rather than gained it. He no longer knew how he was adding value.

A trusted colleague recognized the dilemmas John was facing. This colleague suggested that the two of them stood back from the overflowing inbox. She encouraged John to reflect on the outcomes the laboratory needed to deliver and the most important contribution that John could make to these outcomes. John began to recognize that he had to be more selective about what he got involved in. The laboratory needed him to apply his experience and wisdom to setting the future direction, allocating resources and coordinating the collective effort. It did not require him to be hands-on in leading specific experiments, however much he enjoyed this.

John's experience is mirrored by many individuals who have been promoted into a leadership role because of their technical or professional expertise. A scientist or engineer who is going to be a good leader needs to move from spending most of their time on individual projects to enabling and steering others to lead and manage projects well.

The barrister who becomes a judge has to move on from advocating the causes of individual clients to guiding the thinking of juries and managing the conduct of Court business. The teacher who becomes a Head can no longer spend as much time in the classroom as they used to, because they need to focus on the quality of teaching and learning throughout the school.

Leaders who have been promoted because of their technical and professional expertise can find it hard to let go of the satisfaction of being hands-on. They miss the emotional satisfaction of delivering outcomes themselves and the buzz of personal achievement.

Their other reason for not letting go is that they may believe their expertise is their only source of authority. They are used to being really good at what they do and the wider responsibilities of leadership take them outside of their comfort zone. There is a temptation to stick with the things they know best.

Many well-known leaders have been through this difficult

transition. They have succeeded by asking themselves what they would really like to achieve in their field, and then by challenging themselves on how such achievements are most likely to happen. A classroom teacher can have a huge impact on the year groups who pass through their hands, but a Head can multiply that effect for all of the children who pass through the school. A software engineer can come up with a breakthrough idea, but the head of a team of engineers can work with investors to guide that idea to market.

Ask yourself what true success would look like in your new leadership role. Who are the customers who need to be satisfied about the outcomes you are seeking to deliver? What are the expectations of those who control your budgets and objectives? What do the staff in the organization need from you to enable them to do their jobs to the very best effect?

This analysis is likely to highlight the importance of genuine curiosity in the broader context of your work. The head teacher needs to understand what matters to the governing body and what is influencing parents' choices. The CEO of a software start-up needs to know whether investors and consumers will be receptive to the new idea, or what might make them so. It means acquiring a new type of expertise – and the only way to do it is to leave some of the old expertise to others.

You will develop new sources of authority, deriving from your place in the organization, your understanding of the environment and your access to key decision-makers. Your past sources of authority will still be important, because people will expect to listen to someone with your technical reputation and track record. You will not always be able to give them answers to detailed questions, but your experience will almost certainly equip you to explore their issue with them and give focus to any follow up work by your teams.

Your authority with your teams will also shift in its nature. You might in the past have taken personal satisfaction from being known as an outstanding expert, but what do you want to be known for now? You might want to be known as someone who grows a new set of experts through stretching, mentoring and providing wider perspectives for them to think about.

Your authority is increased if you then allow people to reach their own conclusions having heard your input. If they feel obliged to accept your point of view they may well be reluctant to seek your advice in the future. Standing back may feel hard to do, if your training tells you that there will always be one logically correct answer, which happens to be yours. You may be right but unless the consequences could be catastrophic, you may think it is worth letting them learn the hard way. Besides, many problems are capable of being tackled by more than one route. By listening to others' ideas and encouraging them to develop their thinking, you may open up possibilities that even you had not thought of.

If you want to motivate others to great achievements, it is worth remembering that even the most logical and rational of beings also have emotions that you have to take into account. You may for example be trying to blend a number of solo high performers into a great team. There is plenty of evidence that you are more likely to succeed if they genuinely trust each other and feel a shared passion for the common goal. When you recognize and draw on the strength of those around you, you can build a powerful sense of shared purpose and commitment. People support each other and go the extra mile because they care, not just because they can.

If you as the leader can be a multiplier of energy your authority can be enhanced beyond your initial expectations. The mature leader develops a sensitivity about how they can multiply energy in others, and which of their behaviours risk draining that energy away. They can assess the temperature in an organization, and recognize when they need to galvanize energy, or bring calm to a febrile atmosphere.

After six months in role John had become much more attuned to handling the demands upon him. He had begun to accept that his authority was not dependent on the hands-on leadership of individual experiments. He had learned to appreciate that a thoughtful comment, a key question, or a clear steer, was all that was needed to unblock a situation or shift the way of thinking into a more constructive direction.

John began to take satisfaction in the way he had enabled some of his staff to be more confident in using their strengths and expressing their opinions. John recognized how he had unwittingly diminished the energy and commitment in a particular area because of an unfortunate, off-hand comment. He also recognized how he had raised the level of zest and commitment in other areas because of the steers he had been able to give and the encouragement he had provided for key people. He was glad he had taken the job because he could now see the difference he was making.

For reflection

- What might enable you to appreciate the full range of authority that comes from your past experience?

- What do you want to be known for going forward?

- How might you be a multiplier of energy in other people?

13

Believe you can prioritize

Marcia enjoyed her job as a busy team leader in a local government office. She relished the variety of her work and the mix of activities she was involved in. Marcia prided herself on being able to multitask and handle a range of different priorities over a similar time period.

Marcia's energy and willingness to take on responsibility meant that a wide range of people were making assumptions about what she could deliver. She realized she risked being overwhelmed by her responsibilities and the expectations of others. Somehow she needed to take control – but where to start?

Perhaps you can empathize both with Marcia's excitement and enthusiasm, and her growing apprehension about what she had taken on. You may have had to wrestle with this same tension between being engaged in a range of activities you value and enjoy, while at the same time beginning to recognize the limits on your time and energy.

Your starting point might be that you can see how each task can be done to a high standard. You may be reluctant to delegate as others may not bring the same approach or have a similar focus on consistent quality, but you recognize that unless you delegate more you will have to lower your standards or become so exhausted that you cannot think.

When you recognize you are at risk of being overwhelmed by

conflicting priorities the key questions to ask yourself are: 'what is it that is important and must be done?' and 'what is it that only I can do?' You need to be really strict with yourself on both questions. The first one encourages you to filter out the tasks which could be postponed or even dropped without harmful consequences. The second enables a clear distinction to be drawn between what only you can do, and other things where you can add value but you are not the only person who can take that action. 'What only you can do' might relate to taking final decisions, influencing key decision makers, or making key selection appointments. If you are leading a team, it is less likely to be preparing the first draft of a proposal, or analysing a set of raw data.

It may be helpful to write down your answers to the two questions and ask whether they would convince a neutral observer. Some people find it helps to imagine a glass jar large enough to hold some rocks, some pebbles and some sand. If you fill the jar with pebbles and sand, there is no room to add any rocks. If you start with the rocks, there will be space in the gaps for a modest amount of pebbles and sand. The rocks are the things that must be done and that only you can do.

You could take the analysis further and think about your priorities for, say, the next three or six months, and label your rocks, for example 'oversee the completion of policy papers for the Board', 'manage and develop the team', 'deliver x per cent efficiency savings on the team budget'. If there are too many rocks, or they are too big, you need to ask yourself again, what could be postponed and/or what could be done by others with guidance and coaching.

Proactive management of your time is not selfish indulgence. If you are to serve others effectively, you need to stay resilient and use your time and energy well. If you are clear on your key priorities you should expect the way you use your time to reflect these priorities. Look at your calendar for the period in question. Can you be more systematic in allocating time to match the priorities and more ruthless in declining meetings or email exchanges that add little value? Do you need to block out regular slots for thinking ahead, so that you are not always driven by events?

Few things are more destructive of individuals and teams than a belief that you have to hold on to all your objectives even though it is inevitable that not everything will get done. In these circumstances, it can be helpful to ask sponsors to rank their priorities. You may feel that all the objectives you are addressing are equally important to them, but the thinking of your sponsors may have moved on. Perhaps a project's purpose has been overtaken by events; maybe it was never a priority for more than one or two people. You could even be dealing with colleagues who habitually have ten good ideas in a day, but are genuinely surprised that you are taking all of those ideas equally seriously!

It can be painful to disappoint some people, but it is much better to take control of priorities and have honest conversations with sponsors, than to muddle through and risk not delivering the achievements that really matter.

Another angle is that you may be able to deliver on more of your goals if you judge explicitly and at an early stage how much effort a task really requires. Striving for perfection in everything you do is a worthy aspiration, but exhausting when there are always more priorities than you have time for. Continually asking the question, 'what is good enough?' is a valuable discipline. For example, it must be right to prepare for meetings you are participating in, but not every meeting merits the same investment of time. Sometimes the appropriate preparation is reading lots of detailed papers in advance. On other occasions the most useful preparation is five minutes of personal thought clarifying the two outcomes that are most important for you, and the two contributions you particularly want to make to the discussion.

The influential leader needs to delegate in order to manage their own time and energy – but they also need to do it so that others can learn and grow. Some of the people who work with you may need some steering or encouragement from you before they will take the lead. That should not stop you from delegating, even if your motivation is to protect them. If you hold on to the work, they will never learn, and you will be trapped in a vicious circle where you acquire more and more tasks. It is a key part of the leader's role to make time to coach and develop others. If you ask them, you may find that, far from being grateful for your protection, they are frustrated by the lack of empowerment.

A helpful mindset might be always to ask yourself what would need to happen to enable others to take the lead on a piece of work. If you see success as about developing others to take on your current responsibilities you are both enabling them to develop, and continually renewing your capacity to respond to new expectations. If they do not do the task quite as well as you would, is it still good enough?

Marcia recognized that the financial pressures faced by her local government organization meant that there were ever- growing expectations and fewer people in a position to deliver. A positive consequence was that her colleagues were open to suggestions from her about how tasks could be simplified. Marcia recognized that the more she focused her contribution on effectively progressing a whole programme of business, the more her influence in the organization would grow. This realization gave her the confidence to be blunt that some expectations needed to be changed as they were outdated, of low priority, and unrealistic.

Marcia also became more confident about taking risks in developing others. She had observed a number of people rising into the leadership space after being given more responsibility. She delighted in their success and committed herself to drawing out the best in her people as her top priority, rather than delivering individual tasks herself.

For reflection

- How best do you rank the different priorities that you want to deliver?

- What is it only you can do and how do you ensure enough time and energy to focus on these tasks?

- What is the switch you need to make so you apply the 'good enough' measure rather than a 'perfection' measure?

- What practical steps might you take in managing your diary to use your time and energy more effectively?

14

Learn to engage with 'difficult' people

Manoush was delighted to have been promoted into a team leader role. She had received a lot of encouraging and supportive comments about her promotion. In the first few weeks she had listened carefully and could see the contribution she could make. There was a sense of excitement about the opportunities which this new role provided.

At the same time she felt a growing apprehension about some of the people she now needed to work with. Those same colleagues who had given her words of encouragement were now behaving in a demanding way. Her boss could be challenging and leave her feeling she would never be good enough. People outside the organization had high and possibly unrealistic expectations of her and her team. Manoush began to feel daunted by the prospect of a series of difficult relationships.

Many newly promoted leaders go through similar emotions. There is a combination of excitement and liberation, alongside apprehension and anxiety. The sense of being daunted can lead to viewing colleagues and others with excessive caution or even fear. The risk is that this emotional reaction can dominate your thinking and sap your energy.

A first step is to observe your emotional reaction, detach yourself, and articulate what you think is happening. Perhaps you have observed a similar pattern in past situations and contexts, whether at work or outside of work. What helped you then? Could similar strategies help you now? Perhaps it helped you in the past to discover that the people you found difficult were driven by their own hopes and fears. You may even have discovered when you got to know them that they felt intimidated by you.

With that learning in mind, you could try listing the names and views of those who have an interest in what you do. You may want to draw a stakeholder map, with headings for those you consider to be allies, and those who are opponents or unaware of you. Which of these people are most important for your success and effectiveness? Where does power and authority lie? Who needs to be converted into the ally camp if you are to succeed in your objectives?

An objective analysis of the key decision makers and opinion formers will help sharpen your thinking about where you devote your effort. Whose voice matters? Some players may appear noisy and unhelpful, but their power to derail you may be limited, and it may be more important to use your energies elsewhere.

Having defined who you need to 'get on board', do your homework before you approach them. Find out as much as you can about what motivates them and how others build successful relationships with them.

Talk to people who know them about what matters to them and what success looks like for them. How might you be able to increase their chances of achieving their goals? For example, you might be able to present a proposal to the Chief Executive of a membership organization in a way which anticipates the issues of most concern to their members. Similarly, you might acknowledge up front that a consumer group is right to be angry about poor service quality, rather than go on the defensive. The more that you can stand in the shoes of others, the more they will trust you to be looking for a mutually acceptable way forward.

In dealing with individuals, you also need to think about their personality type, just as you would in dealing with your friends or family members. Some personalities respond best if they are given something to read in advance, so they have time to prepare for a discussion. They may like facts and figures, sometimes in quite a lot of detail.

Other people would definitely not respond well to this sort of approach because they like to agree the headlines and general sense of direction before addressing the details. These people may do their best thinking in a robust exchange of views, and if they challenge you, they expect you to be equally forthright in return. They do not take challenge personally, provided they respect your views. Even in their case, though, it is important to listen more than tell: that is how you pick up the signals on what is most likely to work with this person.

You might conclude that with some challenging stakeholders the relationship is best carried forward by one of your colleagues or one of your team. Where there is already a personal rapport or a shared history there is often no need to disturb that working relationship. On other occasions you might conclude that existing working relationships are too cosy and that you need to be more directly involved, even though that may raise the temperature in the short term.

A clinical look at which relationships need your personal attention is an essential requirement of good leadership. It is right to review this on a periodic basis. What relationships can only you take forward to the next step?

When you feel daunted by someone it is well worth discussing next steps with a trusted colleague. Triangulating your view with others can lead to new insights. Someone might share with you an aspect of an individual's personality and approach which you had not previously understood.

Asking someone to coach you in preparation for a significant conversation with a potentially difficult person can help you develop a plan and anticipate how to respond to their likely reactions. When you have dealt effectively with a couple of challenging relationships in a new role this will help build up your toolkit and confidence for the future.

Becoming less daunted by difficult people involves: knowing your purpose, guarding your emotions, pacing your interventions and keeping your resolve. It helps to review how you have handled difficult conversations effectively in the past, and to ask yourself what stops you from doing this again.

Manoush talked with a peer in the organization about how best to build a good quality working relationship with potentially challenging stakeholders. This helped her put together an approach which was adapted to each key individual. She listed the people she needed to build a strong working relationship with and ranked them in terms of who was most important to the success of her area. She sought to understand her emotional reactions to different people, where those reactions came from, and the strategies that worked best in each case.

Manoush put a plan together which identified when and how she was going to seek to build the right type of ongoing relationships. With some people her approach was to find a task that the two of them could work on together. For others, she looked for shared interests to help build rapport and personal warmth.

Manoush recognized that being curious about what motivated people and why they reacted the way they did was a good place to start. Bringing a sense of curiosity meant she was more likely to smile at the foibles of people rather than feel threatened by them.

For reflection

- What types of people tend to daunt you and how have you handled your emotional reactions to such people in the past?

- Have you got a systematic technique for identifying which challenging relationships need your personal attention?

- How might a sense of curiosity about people help you develop a toolkit for building rapport and a sense of common purpose?

15

Be willing to make decisions

Julia had a key role at a charitable foundation making recommendations about which requests for grants should be approved. Julia loved the work. She was impressed by the passionate commitment of local charities which wanted to change their communities for the better. Julia was inspired by many of the people she met. Virtually every cause seemed well worthwhile.

Julia had two team members who completed the initial screening of the applications against the criteria laid down by the Foundation. Her team would also offer views on the merits of the applications that passed the first screening. The grants requested always exceeded the budget, so Julia's task was to put together carefully argued recommendations for the Grants Committee of the Board. She often thought that all the applications were worthy of support. She would procrastinate and seek further information from the team. Her boss recognized her commitment, but became exasperated when deadlines were not met. The team members and the applicant charities liked Julia's enthusiasm, but were not impressed when they were continually asked for more information, with decisions being deferred.

Julia's boss gave her a clear steer that she needed to be more disciplined in making decisions and living with them.

Most of us want to make the best possible decisions. Some of us are happy to make decisions quickly, either out of instinct or because our job requires it. The fireman who goes into a burning building relies mainly on experience and 'gut feel' to judge when it is no longer safe to remain, and has to make that judgement on the basis of imperfect data. The midwife has to do the same when a mother or baby show signs of distress during the birth. Delay in both cases could be fatal.

Most of the difficult decisions that we have to make at work are not a matter of life or death, and there is always a temptation to put them off in the hopes that extra information will make the solution obvious. Even so, delay can have its downsides.

Crown Prosecutors seek to assemble as much evidence as possible before deciding whether to prosecute. Yet if they leave the decision for too long, the witnesses may drift away and the evidence may get weaker.

The Marketing Director may want to produce a perfect report for the Board on when to launch a new product, and be keen to extend the research beyond their original brief. But the Board may be convinced that delay would lose them competitive advantage.

Leaders can be reluctant decision-takers for a variety of reasons. They may genuinely believe there is such a thing as the perfect answer, when there rarely is. They may use limited information as an excuse to avoid the responsibility of a decision. Or they may habitually avoid committing themselves to anything in life until a hard deadline looms.

We can only make a decision on the basis of the available evidence. In most circumstances, 80 per cent accuracy will be enough, provided of course that it is the right 80 per cent. If you genuinely find it hard to judge, test out your thinking on a few other people and see whether they think any key insights are missing.

If the issue is fear of taking responsibility, others can again help you to weigh up the risks and opportunities inherent in your approach. That does not relieve you as the leader from the ultimate responsibility, but it can allow you to check that you have examined all the angles. It can help you to spot whether your decision risks being compromised by your personal fears or preferences.

You may be one of those people who simply likes to keep their options open for as long as possible. If you are, you may need to remind yourself of the opportunity costs. Whilst this decision remains in your inbox, you may not be giving the necessary attention to several other decisions which are queuing for your consideration. You may be causing huge irritation to the team who are providing you with the data for the decision. They may need to move on to the next priority but keep getting requests from you to revert to this issue. Your enjoyment of the last–minute adrenalin rush may not be a feeling that they share.

The people who are waiting for your decision also deserve your consideration. They have their own needs and priorities to think about. If you are working in a bank and assessing mortgage requests, the applicants would generally prefer a quick answer even if it is no, because they need time to look for other sources of funding.

If you want to make faster decisions you might find it helpful to create some artificial deadlines. For example, you could draft a decision and supporting arguments well ahead of any final deadline, after talking to any colleagues whose input can help you. Then you can put the decision in your drafts folder, dismiss it from your mind and turn to other priorities. A day or two later you can look at the draft again and see how you feel about it. Would you be having second thoughts if you had already sent it? If not, what stops you sending it now?

Similarly, you may be putting off a difficult conversation with someone, perhaps about their performance. If they know the conversation is due, you may be fuelling uncertainty in their minds and damaging their self-confidence. If there is a development message, they need to hear it sooner rather than later so they can do something about it.

What can you learn from observing others who make timely decisions? How do you feel when someone delays a decision that affects you? When have you observed people procrastinating and missing out on great opportunities? Every decision involves some risks that have to be managed, but being indecisive carries just as much risk, if not more.

You almost certainly had the experience in your school or student days of reading an examination paper and feeling uncertain which question to answer. Most of us nevertheless learned to make a quick decision, focus on producing a good answer, and stop thinking about the alternative questions. We knew we could not afford to spend too long worrying about our choices.

Sometimes we have to live with decisions that did not turn out as well as we had hoped. It happens to all of us at some stage. Provided we can tell ourselves that we anticipated the risks and judged them worth taking, we need to look for the learning, and move on.

Julia recognized that she was not helping the applicant charities by delaying her recommendations on which of them should get funding. They all liked her warmth and sincerity but there was a risk she would lose their respect if she kept them waiting for a decision. They knew that not every applicant would be successful. If their request was going to be turned down, they needed to hear quickly so they could apply to other sources.

Julia sat down with her team to look at the shortlisted applications against the aims and objectives of the Foundation. She had a word with a colleague about a couple of cases and shared her thinking about the priorities. Her recommendations were well received by the Board, with a few amendments that gave her insight into their thinking. She gained confidence in her own judgement, and decisions became less challenging with each new round of applications.

For reflection

- What have you learned from observing others who make timely and effective decisions?
- What inhibits you from being decisive and how best do you address those inhibitors?
- What is the way of making decisions that works best for you?

16

Use the power of reflection

Newcomers to Philip's team were surprised that he said relatively little in meetings, and was happy for others to do most of the talking. It looked as though he had no influence, but longer-standing team members knew that Philip would be reflecting on the key issues, and would join in the conversation after he had had the opportunity to reflect. At that point he would summarize what he had heard, and often offer insights and new angles that suddenly took the discussion to a different level.

The difficulty for Philip as a leader was that some colleagues in the wider organization did not know or care how to bring the best out of him. They tended to forget or side-line him, which meant that he and his team were not as influential as they needed to be. Philip could easily get frustrated by the way some people treated him and retreat further into himself. He did not want to become brash and inauthentic, but he knew he had to find a way of being heard.

There is a danger that we have a mental model of leadership as macho, demonstrative and assertive. We hold the picture of a football manager shouting instructions from the touchline, or the business tycoon who ruthlessly squashes the competition.

We may be attracted to leaders who are outgoing, expressive, and always ready to make decisions. Such leaders seem to make things happen by sheer force of personality, and many people are very happy to follow them.

Yet there are drawbacks to this approach. Not everybody wants to be told what to do. Many people at work want to know their ideas will be taken seriously and that they can contribute to decision-making. A more introverted leader (or a self-schooled extrovert) is ready to take advantage of others' input because their ego is less relevant to the decision.

Often the leaders who bring a more reflective approach are better listeners and more responsive to ideas and proactivity from others. They are often better at staying focused on solutions.

They are likely to be more interested in organizational and team success than in personal glory and being centre-stage. They can bring a calm presence in times of stress and are less likely to rush into things and regret their interventions or action. They are more likely to focus on the one-to-one relationships that really matter than to take a scattergun approach to connecting with stakeholders. If you want to know more, try reading Susan Cain's book, 'Quiet: the power of introverts in a world that cannot stop talking'.

Someone who has a natural preference for quiet reflection can bring immense value to a team. They can provide calmness, a sense of focus and recognition of the most effective timing for next steps.

If you are naturally a reflector, celebrate that quality and use it to good effect. Be relieved that you do not have a need to solve a problem instantly. Enjoy the fact that you are good at thinking things through and keeping calm. Choose your moment to intervene but do ensure that you intervene before it is too late.

Build allies who know your qualities and will draw you in. Use your capability of building good one-to-one relationships to create a sense of shared purpose and a mutual willingness to draw out the good qualities in others. Recognize that your lack of ego and willingness to listen may help when there are conflicts to be resolved – and that you are still capable of putting your foot down if you see the need.

You can inspire others just as effectively as those who are more extrovert, through the quality and thoughtfulness of what you say. Think of the public speakers who hold your attention. They are not all showmen. Indeed the flashier performers may prompt your suspicion where the quieter personalities can gain your trust.

There are moments when the leader should be up front sending out a clear message. But the leader who carries conviction will first have set aside good quality reflection time and have thought through what is needed to take people with them.

There are clearly risks to reflecting for too long and either failing to make decisions, or missing an opportunity to influence a debate. That is not what successful reflective leaders do. They weigh up the situation, then judge the moment to make their mark. After a while, others will ask them what they think, because they know their contribution will be worth hearing.

If you are of a more extrovert tendency, you will still benefit from creating space for reflection. All good leaders have either chosen to spend time in a reflective space or have been forced to do so. Jesus would go into the wilderness alone or travel across a lake with his inner group of followers. Nelson Mandela spent decades of forced reflection in prison which changed his whole vision about how to ensure political and cultural change.

It is in periods of reflection that we distil our experience and develop the narrative of leadership we want to take forward. It is only as we stand back that we can reassess and reshape our thinking and ways of being and doing.

Sometimes the power of reflection comes purely through letting the brain process our emotions. Sometimes effective reflection depends on thinking through what has happened and observing how we might have responded differently. Sometimes we are best processing those reflections alone. On other occasions talking with trusted others leads to a breakthrough in our thinking.

Sometimes we learn through reflecting on how we might have handled a situation differently or what might have been the consequences if we had made different decisions at key points. Good quality reflection will look beyond the short-term to assess some of the long-term consequences. Sometimes we will see longer term benefits that we would not have expected.

What is particularly important is deciding what type of reflective space works best for you. It might be a long walk in the hills, or a fifteen-minute walk between meetings, or quiet meditation. What matters is your finding the space and time which enables you to embrace the power of reflection. You then have to find a means of sharing those reflections in a way that is authentic to you and prompts the type of impact you want.

Reflection matters for teams as well as for individuals. All successful teams need to create time for strategic, long-term thinking. That can be easier said than done when there is always so much business to transact and apparently little time to do it. Yet it is essential if the team is not to be constantly in reactive, fire-fighting mode. It can help to be explicit about the need for different types of conversations on different occasions or in different sections of a meeting. Many conversations need to follow an agenda of issues to be progressed and actions to be taken. But effective teams also need to plan regular sessions when they remind themselves about their longer term aims and review the risks and opportunities in the wider environment.

It can sometimes be helpful for teams to mix these approaches and discuss a critical issue twice. In the first discussion there is a reflective consideration of the evidence and exploration of the implications of different types of options. Then in a separate subsequent conversation, there is clearer focus on the decisions that need to be made. This approach may not be possible or desirable before every decision but it is worth considering when a lot rides on the outcome.

Philip knew he had a contribution to make. He realized that he needed strategies to get his contribution heard in the wider organization. He allowed himself time to reflect on the best way of doing this. He decided to approach two or three influential colleagues on a one to one basis and find out what success looked like for them. He soon spotted opportunities to collaborate. He obtained his colleagues' trust by offering ideas that would help them achieve their goals. He then found that they were encouraging him to contribute his ideas in meetings, and creating the space for him to intervene. At the same time he promised himself he would make two or three points at every meeting he attended, and worry less about whether each point was perfectly honed. Over time, those who had previously ignored him became keen to draw out his perspective.

For reflection

- What do you observe about natural reflectors who use this gift to good effect?

- What type of reflection works for you and how do you ensure that the results of that reflection influence next steps?

- How best do you draw out the power of reflection in others and ensure it is influential?

17

Accept you won't always be popular

Helen had always been popular at school and at university. She had a bright and cheerful personality and was never known to upset anyone. After university, she joined a retail firm as a graduate entrant. Her personality and willingness won her many friends and carried her through her junior management roles successfully. When she was promoted to be head of a department, she assumed that everyone would respond to her energy and good humour in much the same way. Yet some of her staff did not respond well to the overtures from this 'bright young thing'. Many of them had long experience in the department and saw no reason to take Helen's leadership seriously.

Staff began to notice Helen did not know how to deal with resistance. She wanted everyone to be nice to each other, and could not exert her authority. They realized they could ignore her when it suited them, and carry on doing things the way they had always done them. Helen was frustrated and upset because she could see the need to improve service quality and was not being heard. A friend from the same graduate scheme pointed out that her desire for harmony was preventing her from confronting issues in the way which was expected of a leader. Helen recognized she needed a radical shift in her approach.

There are many examples of leaders like Helen whose energy

and friendliness only take them so far. They can have a hugely motivating effect on individuals who think as they do, but others need more than enthusiasm for a leader to gain their respect.

Every leader has to accept that they cannot always be popular, especially when they need to make change happen. Leaders are appointed to help their organization achieve its goals and deliver on its objectives. To be successful they need to motivate their people to follow them, and that requires trust and respect for the added value that they bring. They need to show they are approachable, genuine, human beings, but it is unrealistic to expect everyone to like every decision they make.

The most successful sports coaches expect to be unpopular sometimes. Some team members may feel pushed to the edge of their capabilities, and rebellious about the extra training sessions. But if they know that their coach is watchful for their wellbeing, and has led them to success in the past, they will grumble and knuckle down. They would not be impressed by a coach who gave in to the grumbling.

Think about the leaders you have respected. Did you want to know you could trust them, in good times and in bad? Perhaps you did not always feel like living up to their expectations, but you made the effort anyway, because you knew you would learn and grow.

A leader has to bring the best out of others. That means giving everyone a clear sense of direction, and explaining the part that each individual needs to play. If changes are to be made, people need to understand the reasons, and to have these explained in language that makes sense to them.

As an example, you cannot expect to be popular when there are budget cuts to be made, but you will be respected if you take an approach which people feel is fair. It will help if you can involve them in working out the options, and if you can show that you are taking your share of the pain. It will definitely help if you can resolve uncertainty quickly, and show how affected people will be supported. Whatever you decide, some people will not be happy, but that is inevitable.

Each individual in your team needs clarity about your expectations, and regular conversations about their progress. The dialogue is not about the likeability of the other person, but about their ability to do the job they have been hired for. Good performance deserves celebration and should not be taken for granted. If someone is struggling, the leader needs to explore what would help them to succeed, and put the support in place. If they don't or can't take advantage of the support, there has to be a conversation about their future in the job.

When there are difficult messages to be given, it is right to anticipate and plan for the emotional reaction, but it is in no one's interest to be protected from hard truths. Nor is it a kindness to leave someone for years in a job where they will never flourish.

Good quality feedback is a precious gift that enables people to learn continuously from experience. The gift of feedback is not always immediately appreciated, but the recipient may look back in years to come and be grateful that you gave your advice when you did.

Leaders sometimes have to say 'no' to a request or proposal from a team member. Occasionally 'no' must be blunt and unequivocal, in order for it to be taken on board. However, you will get a better emotional response from most people if you give clear reasons, and emphasize that there is no need for this to feel like a personal rejection. They need to hear the message that you value their ideas. The reason why those ideas may not work on this occasion could be all to do with a broader context, and understanding that context will help them to grow in the job.

Do remember to keep affirming people as well as giving the negative feedback. Three points of affirmation alongside one development point is a ratio that often works. If there is a pattern of regular positive feedback, developmental comments are more likely to be received in a constructive way.

Apply the same standards to yourself as a feedback-giver, as you expect of those who give feedback to you. You may resent the boss who comments only when dissatisfied, and regards people as 'too needy' if they want to be told when they are doing well. You may feel they are like a partner who says: 'You know I love you. I would tell you if I didn't.'

A naturally empathetic person has the great advantage that they seek to understand where others are coming from and what their vulnerabilities might be. They then aim to pitch their messages in a way that the other person can hear. Yet our openness to others may not always be returned.

There may be times when we feel someone has taken advantage of our generosity and goodwill. It is easy to feel hurt and rejected, but important to remember you can choose how others' behaviour makes you feel. Even if one person is unreceptive, your reputation may have risen with those who observed you making the effort.

Helen recognized there needed to be a step change in the way she ran the department. She needed to be much clearer about her expectations, and why some practices needed to change. She needed to be more explicit in describing what good performance looked like, then give consistent and specific feedback on what was and was not working.

Helen developed some clear guidelines with her managers about the future direction of the department. They won most people over to their vision, and involved everyone in agreeing the be-haviours that would support success. Helen recognized that she needed to face up to conflict with the resistant minority, rather than avoid it. Her empathetic skills were a great asset in most situations, but she had allowed herself to be too soft-hearted. There would be moments when she would be unpopular, but if she was confident she was doing the right thing for the right reasons, she could live with that.

For reflection

- When are you at risk of not wanting to upset people and how does that distort your approach?
- In what situations are you willing to be unpopular?
- How best can you handle conflict and keep your equi-librium?

18

Manage your emotional reactions

Alwyn was a leader of great ability. He was admired for his skill in getting people's attention and holding an audience. He was quick to recognize team success and generous in hosting celebrations. When he was in a good mood, he was great company. But he could also be short-tempered, and had a reputation for 'not suffering fools gladly'. The people who worked for Alwyn were wary of his unpredictable, darker side which could make him tense and nervous when the pressure was on. They did not fully trust him and were reluctant to share bad news with him or risk taking decisions that might later be derided.

It was only a matter of time before someone took out a grievance case against Alwyn. When he was in a bad mood, his harsh words could be piercing and intimidating, and be felt as bullying. Being the subject of a grievance investigation was a 'wake-up call'. Reading witnesses' descriptions of his behaviour was deeply upsetting, as he did not mean to hurt people.

The investigation ended with a formal warning, and Alwyn recognized that he could not afford for this to happen again. His reputation and possibly his job would be on the line. Following prompting from his senior manager, he commissioned a trusted, independent person to gather confidential feedback from a wide group of colleagues on how they were experiencing him. He knew that the impact he intended to make was not always the impact felt by others. The brutal truth was going to be uncomfortable, but it would give him something to work on. He needed to show he could change.

Sometimes we may be reluctant to put ourselves into stressful leadership situations because we fear we may end up in a similar situation to Alwyn. For some of us, there is a risk of losing our cool and saying or doing something we will regret. As leaders, we know that such actions are very public, and can quickly undermine an otherwise positive reputation. Memories of getting it wrong in the past may lead to a strong desire to avoid pressurized roles where it could happen again.

On other occasions, we may hold back because of past experiences of anxiety and panic attacks. We become anxious about being anxious. As a result, we may miss out on a raft of opportunities to do interesting things and influence other people.

Understanding and managing our emotional reactions is crucial to our success as a leader and our wellbeing. Developing our own self-awareness is a never-ending process as we equip ourselves for a wide range of different situations. Growing self-awareness comes from observing ourselves and, crucially, from finding out how we are perceived by others.

In seeking feedback it is important to include a cross-section of people who are different to you and have emotional reactions that are very different to your own. Resist the temptation only to ask the people who you know will make allowances. Look for patterns in the feedback. Don't become too obsessed with the outliers in the data, but focus on the themes. Try not to become defensive if you see comments which you consider unfair: even if others' perceptions are wrong, you have created these perceptions and you need to address them.

Remember, too, that not everyone feels or thinks like you do. From your perspective, robust criticism of someone else's views may be part of the cut and thrust of intellectual debate, and you don't expect anyone to take offence at forthright language. The other person may come from a culture where such language is considered rude and insensitive. They may feel you are attacking them personally, rather than challenging their ideas.

Once you have the feedback, take time to explore what triggers certain behaviours in you. Questions to ask yourself could include, 'What are the emotional reactions that can entrap me?', or 'What are the emotional reactions that I want to avoid?', or 'What are the early warning signals?' You could have a rich dialogue with a trusted colleague who is willing to ask the same questions of themselves, and who will share their observations of you.

Alternatively, or in addition, you could write your thoughts down and keep developing them over time. What is the attitude of mind you bring to addressing the stressful situations you identify? What type of practical actions work for you and how best do you ensure that you put them into place?

The more we can observe ourselves dispassionately, the more we can develop strategies for spotting the reactions when they are about to happen, and stop them from taking over. Quick-tempered people sometimes talk about a 'red mist' moment when they can't stop themselves letting rip. It is not easy for them to train their brain to take a deep breath, or ask others to excuse them for a moment, but it can be done if the person really wants to change.

You will know from previous experience what can cause a trigger and how you have managed it in the past. What did you learn? Most of us will have taught ourselves some approaches that have worked in at least some types of situation – perhaps within the family or with certain friends. Could that approach, or a variant, work in other types of situation, including at work? Can you also learn from observing others who have a similar make-up to you and appear to manage their reactions well?

You might try focusing for a period on one emotional trigger and developing your capability in handling it. You want to build up new response pathways in the brain. You want to be able to tell yourself stories about how you have successfully handled your emotional reactions and not been obsessed or overwhelmed by them. As you address a particular emotional trigger, recognize that it takes time and practice to change longstanding habits, and be prepared to start with small steps.

For example, if you can lose your cool quickly there is a risk you might send immediate, intemperate emails. A simple step is to put your initial email response into the 'draft box' until you have had time to reflect on its tone and how it might be received by others.

At the heart of our reluctance as leaders is often a fear that we might fail to live up to the expectations of others or the expectations we have set ourselves. We do not want to cause ourselves or others emotional pain. We hold back from situations where we might be frustrated, distraught, cross, and anxious or over stressed. As soon as we hold back we can inhibit the leadership we bring and stunt our growth as leaders.

We are rarely alone in this. We may greatly respect other leaders who share the narrative of their leadership journey, and acknowledge their learning from pain and failure. If we are willing to share our own journey, and are open about a desire to change, we may find that others welcome our honesty, and want to support us.

Alwyn had to steel himself to read the feedback report. He was relieved to see there were many positives about his strong sense of direction and focus on delivery. Yet he was shocked by suggestions of a climate of fear in his team when the pressure was on, and he noted that some colleagues found him uncooperative. The first thing he did was to write to everyone who had contributed feedback, thanking them and being upfront about what he had learned. He arranged to meet some people to seek their views on what he could do differently that would work for them.

Alwyn worked through some psychometric tools with a coach and gained a deeper understanding of his personality. They worked on his emotional trigger points and how he might recognize them in advance. Alwyn became more willing to show his vulnerabilities and seek advice. He planned with more care how to manage his reactions. Although the stories still persisted about his previous moods, he was much more confident of staying in control and being the leader that he wanted to be.

For reflection

- What emotional reactions might be holding you back from realizing your full leadership potential?
- How might you face up to these emotional reactions and develop a plan for managing them effectively?
- If you could manage your emotional reactions more systematically, might that reduce your reluctance to take on bigger leadership responsibilities?

19

Recognize not everyone thinks like you do

Sarah had been Chief Executive of a health charity for a couple of years. She enjoyed the scope this role gave her to plan ahead and set clear priorities. Sarah had spent the first year talking with key partners and leading on the preparation of a strategic plan. Her then Chair had been a wise sounding board but had given Sarah virtually complete freedom to shape the future direction of the charity.

A few months ago a new Chair, Henry, had been appointed. Sarah had assumed there would be a similar relationship to the one with the previous Chair, but soon discovered that Henry would be a very different person to work with. Henry frequently made suggestions. He wanted to make lots of additions to the strategic plan. Henry could always see opportunities which he thought ought to be grasped quickly.

Sarah was finding working with Henry increasingly frustrating. She found she was no longer enjoying leadership like she used to. An observant trustee recognized the potential problems and suggested that both Sarah and Henry do a personality profile assessment. Sarah's preferences were: to think things through on her own, start from the bigger picture, be very rational in her approach and plan ahead carefully. Henry was more spontaneous and he preferred to talk things through as ideas came into his head. He often picked up on an issue of detail and ran with it. He trusted his emotional instincts rather than logic.

It was a 'eureka moment' when the two of them saw that their preferences were opposite to each other. It helped them understand why there had been a degree of frustration in their working relationship. The insight was seeing that their skills and preferences were complementary and that together they could be a strong team. What was needed was for Sarah to recognize the value of Henry's spontaneity and insights, and for Henry to fully support Sarah in her focus on longer term outcomes.

Our starting point is often to believe that life would be much simpler if everyone else thought in the same way as we do, but most successful partnerships or teams include people with a range of complementary skills and preferences.

Good teams benefit from members who have different backgrounds and approaches. Every team needs an optimist who can enable people to think beyond the immediate into what could be possible. A team benefits from having a member who sees the risks and the problems so that they can be properly anticipated.

As you observe different leaders you will see some who are wedded to structure and order, and who find it difficult to be flexible when circumstances require an adaptable response. You will also observe leaders whose natural inclination is to kick against hierarchy and structure, but who need to find ways of making hierarchy work effectively for them.

You may be reluctant to work closely with people who bring a different set of skills and preferences to yours. Success comes from turning through 180 degrees so you become reluctant to work only with people who are similar to you.

If you are reluctant to work with other leaders because they are different from you, it is important to ask yourself why. Is it because you think it will be more difficult to build trust and a close working relationship? Is it unease about how readily you will be able to make joint decisions? Are you perhaps apprehensive about being challenged?

People who find each other 'difficult' often make a breakthrough when they show a genuine interest in what makes each other tick. Having a frank conversation about the approaches that bring the best (and worst) out of each other can lead to valuable insights.

It is helpful to understand what are your natural preferences and what is learned behaviour. We have all developed learned behaviours which enable us to handle a wide range of different situations, despite our initial instincts. However, those instincts can override the learned behaviours in emotional or stressful situations. We can 'revert to type'.

When you work with someone closely it can really help to know whether their approaches and behaviours are deeply rooted in their personality, or whether they flow from learned behaviour. With this insight it is easier to anticipate how they may respond in a crisis or under severe stress.

Recognizing that others think differently to you is particularly important in small teams. For example, in a school the Head and Deputy Head need to understand each other well if they are going to be an effective, complementary team. It is surprising how often there are personality conflicts in a church setting where you might have only two full-time leaders in the vicar and a curate or assistant minister. Where key leadership responsibility is with two people the need for mutual understanding and a recognition of respective roles is even more important than in bigger teams.

The relationship between the Chair and Chief Executive is crucial to the success of any organization. They have very different roles. They need to be able to disagree in private and act as one in public. The Chief Executive needs to recognize their accountability to the Chair but not be overawed by the Chair. There needs to be frankness and mutual respect.

Sarah and Henry worked together pretty well. There were moments when one or two trustees tried to put a wedge between them, but they were astute enough to recognize when this was likely to happen. As Henry fully settled into his role as Chair he felt less need to have a view on everything. He moved more into a strategic space being more selective about how he intervened and on what subjects he took an interest.

Sarah recognized that many of Henry's spontaneous ideas were sound, although they did need to go through a filter of feasibility. Sarah recognized that it was her job to keep coming back to the strategic plan and what was consistent with the strategic plan. But she also recognized that she needed to be adaptable to changing circumstances.

Sarah recognized that she needed to experiment more. She prided herself on her planning, but also acknowledged that as she gained in experience as a Chief Executive she could trust her instincts more and allow herself to be more spontaneous. Sarah came to value Henry's instinct for what people in the organization might be feeling, and how best to engage with them. Henry's approach was gradually rubbing off on Sarah, with her becoming much less reluctant to respond in the moment and follow her insights. She was enjoying leadership again.

For reflection

- Is your natural inclination to work with people who are similar to you or different to you?

- How well do you understand your natural preferences and how marked is your reluctance to act in a way that runs against your natural preferences?

- Who do you need to build a stronger working relationship with who thinks and acts in a way which is different to your approach?

- How might you experiment and be less reluctant to operate outside your comfort zone?

20

Accept your right to be at the table

Josh was appointed to the leadership team in a Government department because of his wide experience outside Government. He was welcomed by his new colleagues who wanted to hear his perspectives. But there were moments when Josh felt like an imposter. This was a bigger job than he had ever done before. His colleagues were much more experienced at working within Government and with Ministers. They were used to working with each other and seemed to talk in code a lot of the time.

Josh oscillated between being confident in his own contribution, and feeling somewhat overawed by his colleagues. On one occasion he was late for a meeting and sat on an empty chair behind his colleagues. The Permanent Secretary immediately asked Josh to come and sit much more in the middle of the group. This slight admonishment from the Permanent Secretary about sitting at the back reminded Josh that he was a full member of the team. His rightful place was fully at the table.

Josh recognized that he had no reason to be overawed by his colleagues. His relative lack of experience was not a good enough excuse for him to sit back and observe. Josh had every right to be at the table and was expected to play a full part. He needed to banish the reluctance that affected him from time to time.

All of us have been in situations where we have felt awkward. We think others know more than we do, have greater experience and insight, and are much more likely to know what is the best course of action. We may feel others are cleverer or more socially adept than we are. Our educational background may be different to theirs and be a cause of a lack of confidence and inhibition.

We risk holding back too much and undermining the contribution that we might otherwise make. As we establish ourselves in a leadership team it is important to listen and observe, but complete silence is rarely helpful. We might begin by asking a few open questions: we might then contribute some reflections from our wider experience. We might spot some consequences that are not obvious to others which it would be helpful to mention. As we understand more clearly the dynamics in a group we might offer to take the lead on a particular issue and thereby be in pole position when it comes to be reporting on progress on that topic.

Key to feeling at home in a leadership team is getting to know colleagues individually and understanding something about their journey and motivation. Looking for common ground and shared interests builds a sense of mutual understanding. Seeking to find opportunities to work in alliance can lead to important breakthroughs in building the right type of rapport with colleagues. Don't let yourself be intimidated by someone's manner: what is important is finding out what matters to the person behind the mask. Meeting your colleagues for coffee or for a meal can build a connection with them as a human being.

When you feel unsure about your place in a team it is worth remembering that you were recruited as the best person to do the job. Your colleagues may well have been waiting for someone with your skills to arrive. You bring experience and achievements that no one else had. There is a distinctiveness about your contribution that no one can take away from you.

Accepting your right to be at the table is about your own self-worth and recognizing what you bring to the team. At a practical level it means reading the papers properly and being ready with the contributions you want to make. It is about positioning yourself in the room so you are able to make eye contact, and so you can hear and be heard. Sometimes you will want to arrive early and develop a rapport with your colleagues before the meeting begins. You may feel less of an imposter if you wear clothes that make you feel confident.

Being fully present and influential in a team meeting involves fully embracing your responsibility to be an active, thoughtful and engaged participant. It means putting away your phone or tablet so you do not look distracted. It also involves accepting the right of other people to be at the table, and demonstrating you are listening and building on what others are saying. The more readily you acknowledge the presence of new team members, the more you will feel fully part of the team.

Accepting your right to be at the table involves being confident in suggesting changes are needed. There may be ways in which the business is conducted that you feel are unhelpful and should be reviewed. It is not your right to demand change but you have as much right as any other member of a leadership team to suggest that certain ways of doing things could be reviewed. It is important to choose your moments to suggest change, but thinking change is needed and failing to make any propositions is a derogation of your responsibilities as a member of a team.

There is an important element of continuous learning. Developing an approach which enables you to have an influential voice in one team helps you with techniques that will apply in other contexts.

If you are in an executive role in a team it is well worth gaining experience in a non-executive capacity, for example in a voluntary organization, to help refine your approach to working in different contexts. Practising the art of being a non-executive director in say, a school, hospital, charity or church will help you recognize you can make a valuable contribution to decisions, even when you have a limited understanding of the details.

Josh kept in his mind the experience of taking the chair behind his colleagues and the gentle reprimand from the Permanent Secretary. He ensured he sat around the leadership table where he could contribute. He was diligent about being fully present and not being tempted to look at his phone. Josh volunteered to be on a range of different groups in order to develop the art of making an impact in a very different setting from his previous world. Josh developed the skill of summarizing at key points in a conversation and drawing out common threads. He soon became recognized as one of the most influential leaders in the organization. Colleagues were now coming to him at an early stage to understand his perspective and to seek his support. He knew he had arrived when others were regularly lobbying him because they recognized the value of his influential voice.

For reflection

- When have you questioned your right to be at the table and how did you address that emotion?

- How do you see your rights and responsibilities as a member of a leadership team?

- How best do you handle occasional hesitancy in exercising your rights and responsibilities as a member of a leadership team?

- What practical steps might you take to enhance your impact so that reluctance to contribute is banished?

21

Do not be overshadowed by your predecessors

Susan had been the incumbent of an Anglican parish church for six months. Becoming a vicar with responsibility for a parish had long been her aspiration. She felt a strong sense of vocation both to be a priest and to have responsibility for a church community. Susan had met her predecessor, Tom, on a couple of occasions and had found his perspective helpful. Tom was clear that Susan was now the incumbent and his focus was on his new and very different parish responsibilities in a neighbouring city.

Susan found that she was wrestling with Tom's legacy. Tom was an inspiring preacher who would always include clear action points in his sermons for his congregation to take forward. Susan's approach in her preaching was more focused on enabling people to think in different ways. Susan sought to enable people to reach their own conclusions in the light of their own interpretation of the relevant biblical passages and contemporary context.

Susan inherited a number of half-completed projects that Tom had initiated, some of which were proving successful while others were struggling. Susan was clear that she wanted to fully respect Tom's legacy, but also knew that she had to prompt fresh thinking with hard decisions needing to be taken about some of his initiatives.

When anyone takes on a new role it is important to reflect on the legacy of their predecessor. It is never helpful to trash the contribution of your predecessor as others may think you will readily criticize them behind their backs.

If your predecessor has left 'under a cloud', you have the advantage of a fresh start. You are able to talk positively about the future and galvanize people into tackling the problems afresh.

Where your predecessor is regarded as a great success, it is right to celebrate the good foundations on which you can build. Proper acknowledgement of what your predecessor has done will reinforce your reputation as someone who cares about the organization more than personal kudos.

When you take over from a successful leader it can feel daunting. There is the nagging doubt as to whether you can do as good a job. There can be a feeling that things can only go downhill. After the initial elation of starting a new role, the shadow of your predecessor can loom large.

What helps are new events. The world does not stand still. The financial situation changes. People leave and other people join. National or local events mean that priorities change. You can guarantee that six months after a respected leader has moved on there will be new challenges which provide opportunities for the new leader.

In any organization some people will be harking back to the glory days of a previous era. There is an inevitability about this which you need to accept, and possibly smile about, in order to minimize your frustration. These individuals can still be motivated to build on past success. It is unhelpful and potentially dangerous to dismiss them as irrelevant, however frustrating some of their attitudes might be.

A key challenge is deciding which of the initiatives set off by your predecessor should be built on further and which might be curtailed. As a newly appointed leader you will often see reality more starkly than those who have been committed to existing initiatives. Your first inclination might be that a particular initiative ought to be brought to an end, but the most productive course of action might be to pose questions and suggest that a review would be timely. You might want to suggest involving others in that review who would bring a fresh perspective. Through the questions you ask and the people you involve, you may find that an initiative that had stalled either gains new momentum, or slowly dies, or becomes subject to scepticism from a number of people and not just you.

The shadow of your predecessor will vary significantly depending on the sector you are in. In many private sector and public sector organizations there is an assumed turnover of leaders which means that the shadow of your predecessor rapidly disappears.

The shadow of the predecessor is particularly acute in charities, churches and other religious organizations, and family businesses. If someone has built up a charity they may well feel a strong sense of oversight for its future wellbeing which can be unhelpful for the successor. In churches and other religious organizations the personality of the leader may well have shaped the way an organization behaves. The leader will normally have moved on, but their acolytes who are still within the organization may suffer from long-term bereavement which inhibits their support of the next leader.

In family businesses the previous Chief Executive may now be chair of the Board or a non-executive on the Board and still have a significant, financial interest. Someone might have been groomed to take over a family firm but can find themselves overawed by the continued presence of the family member or members who founded it. What is vital in such situations is clear contracting between the current leader and their predecessors so the current leaders are allowed to lead whilst periodically seeking the advice of the family members.

Succeeding someone who is regarded as a giant is daunting. The risk is that you freeze and want the tacit approval of your predecessor before taking action. You might hold in your mind's eye a mental picture of your predecessor and be asking yourself whether they would approve of your decisions. What matters is that you are now the leader. You have been chosen to hold the leadership responsibilities. You are accountable for your actions, not your predecessor.

When you feel overawed by your predecessor it can be helpful to remember that no leader is infallible. Giants often have 'feet of clay'. Seek to be as objective as you can about the pluses and minuses of the legacy of your predecessor, and recognize what might be the changes and developments that are essential for the organization to move forward. When you are honest about how best you need to move on from a previous legacy, you can build the confidence to move out of the shadow of your predecessor.

Susan had a two-day silent retreat after six months in the role as vicar. She listed all of Tom's achievements which she wanted to build on, and the initiatives she might not pursue. Susan was clear that her approach to preaching and leading needed to be authentic to her personality and calling, and to the needs of the community of which she was now part. Susan recognized that she needed to 'get a grip on her reluctance' and move out of the shadow of her predecessor.

Susan committed herself to having constructive conversations with her church wardens (the senior lay leaders in the church) and her staff team about the way ahead. Susan felt that she had crossed a watershed and was ready for the next phase. She was comfortable in herself as an enabling leader and could admire Tom without feeling the need to imitate him.

For reflection

- How are you responding to the shadow of your predecessor?

- How best do you ensure that you are not captured by the legacy of your predecessor while building on the firm foundations which they constructed?

- How fully have you embraced your own authentic leadership approach uninhibited by the shadow of your predecessor?

22

Know what keeps you fresh and energized

Clare's parents were both teachers who were fulfilled in their work. In her teenage years, Clare had taught in the Sunday school and had been the Snowy Owl in the local Brownie pack. It was natural for her to train as a primary school teacher. She enjoyed teaching practice at a range of schools during her training and was quickly established in her career.

Clare's energy and commitment showed through clearly. Before long she was a Deputy Head and then was appointed Head of a Church of England primary school in her early thirties. Clare relished the responsibilities as Head and built up a strong team. Hers was a popular school with committed, if somewhat demanding, parents.

In her first five years as Head, Clare made the changes she wanted and delighted in the progress of the school. But she was getting frustrated by form-filling and bureaucracy which seemed never ending. The school inspections seemed to her to focus too much on detail rather than the overall impact of the school. Some frustrations with staff attitudes began to sap her energy.

Clare was conscious that her fortieth birthday was not long away. She recognized she had had a successful and fulfilling first half of her career, and was wondering where it would go next. Her zest for leadership had taken a knock over recent months, but she continued to have a strong desire to keep learning and growing. The question was how did she draw out that desire and move creatively into the next phase, keeping herself fresh and energized?

Clare is an example of someone who may have peaked relatively early in their career. Sometimes you can be in the right place at the right time and move almost seamlessly into senior posts. The thrill of being fulfilled and successful takes you quickly to a point which many people do not reach, or only attain much later in their working life. You bring energy and youth uninhibited by the ups and downs of wider experience, but all of a sudden you can feel stuck and unsure about the future.

You work hard to make certain that your organization, or your part of an organization, is working well, but then you are hit by circumstances beyond your control. Your immediate boss might change and bring a very different set of aspirations. You might lose some key people and find recruitment not as easy as you had thought. External inspection or review might cast doubt on the effectiveness of your leadership. The financial situation might go contrary to your expectation.

You can find yourself going from 'boom to gloom' surprisingly quickly. It is as if the foundations you had built are not nearly as robust as expected. You need to readjust your priorities and expectations in a way you had not anticipated.

When your leadership is going well it is always worth spending some time considering the risks and seeing how you can forestall potential problems. Succession planning for future posts can help prepare for unexpected changes. Building sustainability in the way resources and energy are used can help prepare for future shocks.

It is worth considering your plan 'B' in case there are unexpected developments which mean you have to think about moving on.

It is always worth thinking through in any leadership role what is keeping you fresh and energized. Are you in dialogue with people in different leadership roles with whom you can share ideas and seek to understand what works for them.

When you feel too busy to take part in continuous learning and professional development it is time to readjust your priorities and think afresh about how you want to keep up to date and professionally stimulated. Reflect on who you spend time with who stimulates your curiosity and enables you to think in constructive and creative ways. Two hours in dialogue with someone who helps you think creatively can provide an energy flow that will keep you going in tough weeks.

For some, keeping fresh and energized is about creative dialogue with trusted colleagues and friends. For others, freshness and new energy comes through time reflecting and meditating – which might be on a structured retreat or through guided reading or on a long walk. A time of peaceful meditation might be when you are sitting on a commuter train for forty minutes or when driving home from work after a busy day.

Freshness and energy in work is linked to what keeps you fresh and energized outside work. Keeping up your vitality outside work might involve spending time with the children in your lives, or reading articles and books far away from your professional realm, or physical pursuits that fully absorb your mental and emotional faculties as well as your limbs. Being deliberate about how you keep fresh and energized equips you to handle the inevitable ups and downs of your journey in your work.

As leader you have a responsibility to those around you. If you are energized, they are likely to follow that example. If you begin to lose some of your zest for the shared endeavour this mood might be passed on. You risk becoming a drain rather than a radiator. Whatever you feel inside, you need to keep your doubts to yourself if you want to avoid having a negative impact.

One way of working through a low point in your own experience is to coach others who feel stuck in their own professional or personal lives. You may choose not to share your own story, but the process of coaching may help you to see your own way forward.

When you think that you might have peaked, with your zest for leading being diminished, be open-minded about what the future might hold. We do not know what might be round the corner. The best may be yet to come. There might be new opportunities within your particular area of work, or perhaps the generic skills you bring could be applicable in other areas.

If you have worked in the private sector, might you consider working in the public sector or for a charity? If you have done a specialist role, might you consider moving into a general management role? Might you consider doing a course that will equip you with a new set of skills? Perhaps there is an opportunity to do a programme at a college or university that might widen your horizons and open up new possibilities?

Clare recognized that now was the right time to be thinking about her next phase. There was still much to be done at the primary school where she was Head: there was at least five years more work there that would be fulfilling. Nevertheless, it might be time to think about applying to be Head of a larger primary school or to work in teacher training.

Clare was conscious that she needed to develop her leadership resilience and could learn from talking with leaders in other spheres.

She enrolled in a continuing professional development programme at the local university. Clare decided to join a local choir as she found music absorbing. She decided to be part of a team working with older people at her church which would provide a complete contrast to her work with primary aged children.

Clare recollected the inner confidence that had allowed her to progress quickly to become a primary school Head. Clare wanted to nurture that same confidence to take her into different spheres and to enable her to be open-minded about her own next steps.

For reflection

- Can you express dispassionately where you are on your career path and what is important to enable you to stay fresh and energized for the future?
- How best do you maintain a level of self-awareness so you are conscious of the impact you are having on others and whether any negative emotions might be contagious?
- How do you respond to the comment that, 'the best could be yet to come'?
- How might curiosity about the future keep you fresh and energized?

23

Inspire the hesitant

Mo was relishing his new role as IT Director for a growing restaurant business. He loved being a member of the executive team and seeing how his department played a critical role in a success story. He was asked to brief the Board on the implications of a takeover bid for a similar sized business and saw some great opportunities. He wanted and needed to play a key part in managing the change programme if the deal went ahead.

However, Mo knew he would be severely stretched by the workload, because his two deputies showed no sign of wanting more leadership responsibility. Mo thought he had made it clear he was keen to delegate and empower them, but he could not extricate himself from day-to-day operations. Other departments still brought all their service issues to him, and his deputies made no effort to change that. He could not understand their reluctance, as in their place he would have been champing at the bit.

It is frustrating when you are held back in your own leadership ambitions by the reluctance of others to step up. Sooner or later, every leader has to help others to lead. The key is to recognize that they may not tick the same way as you do.

This book has been exploring the many reasons why people may be reluctant to fulfil their leadership potential. You may make assumptions about what is holding a colleague back, but you could be completely wrong. The best way of finding out is to ask them, but a boss who asks the question head on may hear what the other person thinks they want to hear, rather than the real answer.

There needs to be some trust in the relationship – best achieved by the senior leader showing a genuine interest in their colleague as a person, and giving them time for one to one conversations which are not just about a list of tasks to be done.

It is a good idea to start by finding out about this colleague's aspirations in work and in life. In most cases you will find that they would like to advance their career at some stage, whether for job satisfaction, status or financial security. It may not have struck them that they are more likely to gain promotion if they show willingness to take on extra responsibility at their current level. Alternatively, they may recognize this, but feel they are not yet ready. Responsibility carries risks, and they may not have the confidence to grasp the opportunity.

You might explore with your colleague what support they would need, to enable them to step up with confidence. Remember, different people may need different types of support. One person might ask to shadow you when you meet colleagues they are anxious about, so that they can see how you build productive relationships. Another might ask you for feedback on how they come across in meetings. A third might need your reassurance that you will back them if a calculated risk does not pay off.

If someone seems stricken by self-doubt, you may need to encourage them to spend time writing down all their strengths in relation to what needs to be done. Don't allow them to talk about weaknesses until they have written down their strengths. Then ask them what it would take to address any weaknesses, and whether there are others in the team who have balancing strengths to draw on. It is rarely necessary – or possible – for a complete suite of talents to be located in one person. Your colleague's greatest development need may be to learn how to build a team around them.

Be aware that there may be cultural issues underlying their reluctance. Your colleague may come from a background where hierarchy is important and using personal initiative is frowned upon. You may need to explain with appropriate sensitivity that your workplace welcomes and encourages self-starters.

Coaching and developing direct reports is one of the most important parts of the leader's role, because no one else is going to do it. It does mean investing time, but without that investment, their potential may be wasted, and you may not have the space to achieve yours.

Coaching requires open questions and excellent listening skills. It also means giving the other person time to think about your questions. Do not be tempted to fill every silence by asking another question. If you allow the other person to reflect without interruption, you may gain valuable insights when they eventually speak. When you do ask another question, you can build on what they have just said, and gain even more insight.

What if someone does not respond to your encouragement, however hard you try? You will want to check whether a different approach is needed – perhaps by consulting a colleague on how they would engage with this person. If that takes you no further, you need to take a view on whether the individual lacks motivation, or is genuinely unable to respond.

You may then need some frank conversations with the individual about your expectations of the role they occupy. It is possible they have assumed their objectives are only about task delivery and have not appreciated that leadership behaviours are part of the package of expectations. You owe them complete clarity. Often that is enough for the person to take the support on offer and make the effort that is needed. If they just can't rise to the challenge, it is much better to face the facts with them, than to let the situation fester. Treat them with respect, and help them look for roles which may suit them better.

When Mo heard that the takeover deal was going ahead, he knew he had to talk to his two deputies, Nick and Geeta, about his expectations of them. Mo would need to focus on the integrated systems strategy for the new business, and they would need to keep existing services running to the satisfaction of internal clients. He briefed Nick and Geeta together about the changes, but then arranged longer one to one conversations with each of them. In each case, Mo explained what he needed of them, and asked how they felt about it.

Nick revealed he was nervous about dealing direct with senior colleagues in other departments, because they could be very demanding, without understanding the competing pressures on Nick's team. Nick had always been relieved to leave Mo to handle these relationships, and had accepted the implication that his own career might be stuck as a result. It had not occurred to him to ask Mo for some coaching. He began to accompany Mo to meetings with the most demanding stakeholders, and learned the approaches that worked with each of them.

Geeta thanked Mo for the opportunity to take a more prominent role, but said she did not feel ready. Mo suppressed the thought that she was perfectly capable and just needed to get on with things. Instead, he encouraged her to talk about what the role needed, and how her strengths matched. He gave her time to unpack what was holding her back, and to identify the type of support that could help. After two or three conversations, it became clear that Geeta wanted a safe space to share her ideas and feelings when the going got tough. Mo agreed to find her a mentor or coach, and that gave her the confidence to step forward.

For reflection

- As a leader, are you recognizing your responsibility to help others to step up?

- Are you sufficiently curious about why they might be reluctant leaders?

- Are you developing your listening and coaching skills, to help them move forward?

24

Coach your team to lead

Ade had been Chief Executive of an online business for just over a year. She had inherited two Directors with strong potential, and two who needed to move on. She was pleased with the two new appointments she had made, and could see each of the four departments responding well to a challenging environment.

Ade nevertheless felt that the business was not getting full benefit from all these capable individuals. When her Directors met the non-executive Board they each talked about their own areas but there was no sense of them being joined up. They appeared to rely on Ade to provide the strategic overview, and also to be the voice of the organization with the staff and key stakeholders. She wanted them to understand that each of them had a role in leading the whole organization.

Leaders in all types of organization face the same question as Ade. They want to harness the different skills, abilities and personalities of their top team members so that the whole adds up to something greater than the sum of the parts. This rarely happens without positive encouragement and coaching. Whatever the day-to-day pressures, it is worth investing time in talking to each team member on their own, and then in discussion as a group.

A starting point is for the team to ask itself what it could achieve for the organization by working together and pooling their thinking.

The joint activities which tend to get mentioned are about shaping the strategy, agreeing how the elements of the corporate plan fit together, allocating resources and monitoring delivery. These areas are all critically important, but are often tackled by the team in a confrontational way, leaving the leader to decide between competing arguments.

If a team is to take ownership of the decisions, the members need to care more about the success of the organization, than about their individual success. This is a big ask, but this is the mindset each of them will need if they are to take the top job one day.

Ideally, the group should discuss what stops them from getting the best out of each other. This requires a significant degree of mutual trust, and may not happen at the first attempt. The leader may want to open the way by sharing what brings out the best and worst in them at work, and seeking feedback on how the others perceive them.

Sharing personality profiles (such as Myers Briggs) is a low-risk approach to getting the conversation started. A typical example is when one person admits they sometimes speak without thinking whilst another recognizes they think for so long that they sometimes never speak at all. Just getting that out on the table can lead to a productive conversation.

Another exercise involves inviting each person to write down, anonymously if they wish, how they would describe the team at its best, and what characterizes it at its worst. The discussion then explores what it would take for the team to be at its best more of the time.

For example, a frequent comment is that team members come to a meeting with their minds made up on an issue. Their focus is on how to win the argument and they have no interest in listening to others' contributions, let alone being persuaded to change their mind. The decision may be dictated by the loudest voice rather than careful reasoning, sometimes with far-reaching consequences. Recognizing this is happening is the first step towards agreeing a better way forward.

Better team collaboration is not an end in itself. It is a means to getting the collective job done. In discussing their best and worst behaviours, the team may recognize that their shared responsibility goes beyond producing corporate plans. They need to inspire the whole organization to support the vision, and to work across functional boundaries to deliver it.

The team needs to work together on a compelling story about the organization's future. They each need to commit to supporting the collective narrative when they are out of the room. They should anticipate what people will worry about, and agree how to respond to challenge.

Similarly, the team needs to discuss the key stakeholders for the organization, and the arguments that will be influential with them. Different audiences will need different approaches, depending on what they care about, but the overall narrative needs to be consistent, or external reputation will suffer.

The team leader takes a full part in this work, whilst at the same time creating expectations of each of the others. Team members should be in no doubt that they will be judged by their wider corporate contribution as much as by their functional role.

The team leader may reinforce the message by delegating leadership of an issue to two or more team members who are not known for collaborating. They may encourage pairs to lead road-shows with employees in each others' areas, or to lead a joint dialogue with managers at the next level.

If you think this is unrealistic, try asking a few people you know about the best team they have ever known, whether at work or in their outside life. Encourage them to talk about how it felt to be part of that team. The odds are they will talk about a sense of being 'in it together', 'committed to each others' success' and 'having a shared passion'. Words like 'trust' and 'mutual support' usually come up, and people nearly always say that, however tough the challenge, they were sorry to leave.

Ade decided it was time to appoint an external coach to work with her and the team. She emphasized that she thought highly of each team member and her decision should not be taken as criticism. Her point was that, at a time of severe external pressures, the team needed to be the best it could possibly be.

Before the first team event, Ade asked the coach to speak individually to each member of the team, to the Chair of the Board and to a group of managers at the next level. The coach asked what was good about the team, and where it could be better. The coach anonymized the feedback and presented it at the team event.

It became clear that everyone recognized they were not functioning as a team, except at the mechanistic level. Some people quite liked being left to themselves, but even they recognized that it was not good for the organization. It particularly struck them that neither the Board nor the middle managers saw them operating collectively. They also realized they were often diverting Ade's energies into acting as referee or adjudicator.

These were uncomfortable truths for a group of people with high ambitions. They decided that something had to change, and set about working with Ade on what that might look like.

For reflection

- Does your team know what it must do together, that cannot be done by individuals acting separately?

- Does each team member understand what you expect of them as a corporate leader?

- Are you ready to coach the team and lead by example?

25

Decide on your next steps

1. Become aware of how your brain works, especially that the rational brain needs time to catch up with your emotional responses.

2. Bring clarity to your feelings by writing them down, or talking to someone else about them.

3. Confront your fears and the likelihood of them materializing.

4. Be honest with yourself about your strengths as well as your blind spots.

5. Work out where others are coming from and what success looks like for them.

6. Accept that not everyone thinks like you, and draw strength from diversity.

7. Know and use your sources of support.

8. Use your time where you can add most value.

9. Recognize what keeps you fresh and energized.

10. Know what renews your sense of purpose or vocation.

The right next steps will be personal to you. We encourage you to reflect on which chapters of the book have spoken particularly to you and how you are going to take forward new or refreshed insights. What are the themes that are especially pertinent for you as you look forward?

We encourage you to write down ten insights that you can turn into practical steps. On the previous page are ten steps that seem especially important from our observations.

When you have decided on the right ten next steps for you, try talking them through with a couple of friends and colleagues. Invite them to encourage you and to hold you to account. Then, in a few months' time, review your progress and update your ten steps. It takes time to change longstanding habits, so don't expect instant results – but you may be pleasantly surprised by the progress you have made.

Further reading

If this book has made you curious to explore some issues further, you might like to try the following books.

Susan Cain, *Quiet: The Power of Introverts in a World That Can't Stop Talking*, Penguin, 2013.

Carol S. Dweck, *Mindset*, Random House, 2006.

Eric Berne, *Games People Play*, Penguin, 2010.

Nancy Kline, *Time to Think*, Cassell, 1999.

Steve Peters, *The Chimp Paradox*, Vermilion/ Ebury Publishing, 2012.

David Rock, *Your Brain at Work*, HarperCollins, 2009.

Peter Shaw, *Getting the Balance Right*, Marshall Cavendish, 2013.

Peter Shaw, *Wake Up and Dream: Stepping into Your Future*, Canterbury Press, 2015.